1111 Days In My Life
Plus Four

Donated by

Merrill Leffler
of
Dryad Press

1111 Days In My Life Plus Four

Ephraim F. Sten

Translated from the Hebrew by Moshe Dor
Foreword by Myra Sklarew

Dryad Press
In Association with the University of Wisconsin Press

Printed in the United States of America

Cover photograph: "1933 Metz, France," by Marcel Bardon
Text and cover design by Sandy Rodgers

Text is typeset in Minion: 11 over 13.5 italic (original journal entries) and 11 over
13.5 display (present day entries)

The paper used in this publication meets the minimum requirements of American
National Standard for Information Sciences — Permanence of paper for Printed
Library Materials, ANSI Z39.48

Dryad Press
P.O. Box 11233
Takoma Park, Maryland 20913
dryadpress@yahoo.com

1111 Days in My Life Plus Four is distributed to the trade by the University of
Wisconsin Press, 1930 Monroe Street, 3rd Floor, Madison, Wisconsin 53711-2059,
www.wisc.edu/wisconsinpress

LIBRARY OF CONGRESS CATALOGING-IN-PUBLICATION DATA

Sten, Ephraim.
   1111 days in my life plus four / Ephraim F. Sten ; translated from the Hebrew by
   Moshe Dor ; foreword by Myra Sklarew.
   p. cm.
   English translation from Hebrew of a work originally in Polish. Includes bibliographi-
   cal references and index.
   ISBN 1-928755-08-9 (pbk. (smythe-sewn) : alk. paper)
   1. Sten, Ephraim—Diaries. 2. Jewish children—Ukraine—Zolochiv (L'vivs'ka
   oblast')—Diaries. 3. Sten, Ephraim—Childhood and youth. 4. Holocaust, Jewish
   (1939-1945)—Ukraine—Zolochiv (L'vivs'ka oblast')—Personal narratives.
   5. Holocaust, Jewish (1939-1945)—Ukraine—Zolochiv (L'vivs'ka oblast')—Personal
   narratives—History and criticism. 6. Holocaust survivors—Israel—Tel Aviv—
   Biography. 7. Zolochiv (L'vivs'ka oblast', Ukraine)—Biography. 8. Tel Aviv (Israel)—
   Biography. I. Title: One thousand one hundred eleven days of my life plus four.
   II. Dor, Mosheh, 1932- III. Title.

   PJ5055.42.T46Z43   2005
   892.4'8703—dc22   2005011693

To the memory of my father

Contents

Foreword

Ephraim Sten, born in the town of Zloczow, Poland, and in hiding during World War II for three years beginning when he was thirteen, did eventually return to the town of his birth. In a sense, he had been returning for years. In memory: "A German officer, tall polished boots, his gun pointed at a big-eared boy in short pants. The boy is running into an alley. On the right, a rough clapboard fence . . ." And in the physical reality: ". . . how nice to find the fence still standing, as if remembering my athletic feat."

Ephraim Sten kept a journal during the war years. As an adult in Israel in the 90s — because his children wanted to read his diary, to know what their father had experienced — he began to translate the diary from Polish to Hebrew. And in the course of this work, the adult began to respond to the entries he had made as a youngster. What we have is a remarkable double testimony — the adult reaching back across the years of his life to the boy he had been to create a dialogue. Moshe Dor, a leading Israeli poet and friend, translated the diary into English. Thus, the work the reader finds here has been transfused through three languages, three separate cultures, through war and peace and war.

The adult is unsparing in his words to the boy he was; yet the boy too speaks of having only one asset: "exaggerated self-criticism." The boy who speaks from these pages is astonishingly learned, fully conscious, his observations unique: "Jews have always been liquidated. . . . Who are we anyway? A comma in History." He muses on the terrible irony that Chmielnicki exists in history because of the "thousands of Jewish and Polish victims that he slaughtered. . . . Hitler, too, will enter History because of us." And the adult is equally critical of his own motivations. "The diary," he writes, "is supposed to remind one of that cliché . . . about the phoenix rising from its ashes. What becomes clearer and clearer in this writing is that the ashes are the end. . . . The writing was supposed to be a contribution to memory, recycling a dark period in life, but in retrospect, I'm convinced it was born by mistake. For decades I was not conscious of the load crushing my soul. This damned writing has newly rediscovered everything."

Ephraim Sten's actual return to Zloczow gives credence to the fact that he had once lived in that place, that the adult hadn't invented it. Writing about this, the adult becomes real to himself and to the possibility that some "trace" of him will remain.

The Polish poet Tadeusz Rozewicz once wrote:

> Forget about us about our generation
> live like human beings
> forget about us
>
> we envied
> plants and stones
> we envied dogs

Ephraim Sten, in his journal written between the years 1941 and 1944, speaks of envying the chickens in the yard their freedom, or the dog he embraces who "smells of fields, forest, wind." As an adult he speaks of the Tel Aviv he loves, for knowing that at any moment he can go out, "enter anywhere" he wishes. Here he sympathizes with Anne Frank, "the girl imprisoned in her room, unable to move about, bereft of Man's basic right: Freedom." He tells of the terrible passivity required during hiding: "in a grave-like pit, narrow and long," eight people locked into a small space, in pairs, without being able to speak for many hours at a time — "boredom, darkness, hunger." Germans living virtually in the next room in the same house.

There comes a moment, after an altercation among those living so closely together, when Sten contemplates leaving, simply walking away. "When I was a child I saw a man drowning. He was swimming in the river and suddenly it seemed somebody was pulling him by his leg. He waved his arms, he might have cried out, and then disappeared in the deep." The adult Sten acknowledges that this memory likely indicates that had he actually left, he would have been killed. He jokes then about the "terrific" posthumous "finish to [his] diary." Plays, translations, royalties. But alas . . . the money wouldn't flow into his pockets because he hadn't any pockets!

In dreaming, the role of the body is stillness while the role of the dreamer is to wander about in the world, backward and forward through time with no limitation. In hiding, the body like that of the dreamer's must be completely still; yet the mind of the hidden one is acutely attentive, vigilant for any sound that could result in his discovery and death.

Vamik D. Volkan, in "After the Violence," writes about "perennial mourning" where those who have suffered trauma postpone completion of the mourning process. They employ what he terms linking objects, "a mental meeting point between representation of the deceased and the corresponding self-image of the mourner" — a letter, a piece of clothing, a watch. Though linking objects can be used to postpone the mourning process, they can also be used adoptively to initiate future mourning when the mourner has the emotional resources to confront the loss. The small journal kept by Ephraim Sten during his years in hiding, replete with intricate architectural drawings, became such a linking object. It forms the basis for the dialogue between the adult and the child he had once been.

Elie Wiesel once said that when the voice of the child he had been before the War coalesces with the voice of the man he is now, he begins to hear the first words of his novels. What has been vanquished is his adolescence. Across the chasm of the Holocaust, the man meets once more the child he was. Together, united, integrated, the man can begin to speak.

However, whether there can ever be full integration is a question. Whether the experience of the Holocaust can be made to reside within a later "normal" life is doubtful. Hiding presents unique problems for a child. As Alan Berger writes in *Jewish American and Holocaust Literature: A Late Twentieth-Century Look*, "reconstructing fragments of memory which, while bringing cohesion to their experience, also causes great pain as the hidden children remember parents and other relatives who were murdered in the Holocaust. Furthermore, public ignorance of, and silence about hidden children, meant non-validation of the experience of the youngest survivors of the Shoah. It was as if they had been expelled from the history of the Holocaust." In some cases, continued silence after the War was essential because the families that hid Jews could be endangered by their neighbors were it known that they had sheltered Jews. And perhaps the most serious aspect of hiding, apart from the daily mortal threat, was the necessary denial of all that a child was: a child with the right to live as anyone else, a child with a mother and father, siblings, a Jew. This kind of negation cannot simply be erased at the moment when hiding is no longer a necessity.

The reader of this book might feel that the author has come to some catharsis: Ephraim always made it clear to his family that he could not. Over the years, he always stressed his reservation about the term attached to him and others as Holocaust survivors (nitzolim in Hebrew). He said there were/are no survivors (in Hebrew the word comes from the root "to save/rescue"), only remnants, remains (s'ridim in Hebrew). He brought up his children to believe that one couldn't become whole after such an experience; one is always damaged goods. He emphasized this over and over again — one could not be rescued, which included the healing of old wounds, not from the Holocaust. There is no closure, and in the eyes of his family, Ephraim never reached one — neither through the first translation of the diary into Hebrew, nor through the visit to Zloczow, nor through writing the book.

In the pages of Ephraim Sten's journal, *1111 Days in My Life Plus Four*, the adult man meets once more the boy he had been during the Second World War. At times there is an infinite distance between the boy and the man. At times they are side by side. At times they cross over into one another. And at times they exchange places.

Ephraim Sten had the opportunity to see again one of those who saved him, Hryc Tyz. "You are my relatives," Hryc told him.

"The Jews I had saved scattered all over the world. . . . I didn't believe I'd be lucky to yet see somebody from my family." Sten never forgot those who had saved his life at great risk to their own, their families, their communities, helping them over all the years that remained to him. In addition to Hryc Tyz, Helena Skrzeszewska and Misia Koreniuk worked to save Ephraim Sten and the others. We say their names, as Ephraim would have wished it.

Near the end of his journal, Ephraim writes:

> In the epic of his wanderings, Ulysses once sat at the entrance of the Underworld and waited for the soul of his departed friend. He had a slaughtered ram at his feet because its fresh blood had the virtue of reviving consciousness. Around him swirled and pushed multitudes of the dead who also wanted to gain a moment of resurrection. But Ulysses was determined not to let them approach. He arrived from far away and was waiting for only one soul.
>
> In this writing I am both Ulysses and the slaughtered ram. My own blood revived several ghosts and like Ulysses I kept my right to choose. The ghosts that were no part of the diary crowded round my puddle of blood, but I spurned them and didn't let them have another transformation. That was my privilege — as in Homer's metaphor — of emotional and intellectual choice. Possibly the others' turns would have arrived if I had allotted myself enough time. But now I'm bidding farewell to the voices, faces and images to which I haven't brought life but my dreams were overflowing with them for a long time.

In this extraordinary work, at last, the boy who suffered confinement and lack of choice and daily mortal threat at a time when youngsters are keenest to explore the world, and the man he became — wanderer and source of consciousness — though never fully integrated, finally stand side by side in an attempt to free themselves from the voices, faces, images of their shared past.

Myra Sklarew
Bethesda, Maryland

Zloczow and the German Occupation

Zloczow dates back as a village in Galicia to the mid-15th century, gaining the status of a city in 1523. It was annexed by Austria in 1772 and only became part of Poland for 21 years, beginning in 1918. The Soviet Union then grabbed Zloczow, which is now in the Ukraine (spelled Zolochiv). Accounts of Jews living in Zloczow go back at least to the 16th century, though the beginnings of a Jewish community were in the early 17th century: a wooden synagogue was first built in 1613 and a cemetery established. Between 1880 and 1921, Jews constituted nearly 50 percent of Zloczow's population that averaged nearly 11,000. In 1939, the number of Jews swelled to some 14,000 after Germany occupied western Poland and the Soviet Union had seized Zloczow. When Germany invaded the Soviet Union on June 22, 1941, only a small number of Jews managed to escape further to the East.

The German occupation of Zlozow began on July 2, 1941. With many local Ukrainians and farmers flooding into town to welcome them, the Nazi SS instigated a devastating pogrom that lasted for three days. It resulted in the deaths of 3,500 Jews. Ephraim Sten's father himself was shot and left for dead — he was able to crawl out with the help of two friends. The thirteen-year old Ephraim wrote in his new diary on July 6th, *"Around three o'clock they shot Father, but as he happened to already be in the ditch, all four bullets hit the pile of dirt, and Father fell down and pretended to be dead."*

In this first month, the SS established the local Judenrat — the Jewish Council like others the Germans established in occupied territories to carry out their orders in Jewish communities. Headed by Zigmunt Meiblum, a community leader and former head of the local Zionist organization, the Judenrat was charged with carrying out such demands as supplying manpower for forced labor and collecting valuables of all kinds for delivery to the Germans. Ephraim began working as an errand boy for the Judenrat: *"to be more precise,"* he wrote on August 14th, *"I run all the time."* The Judenrat's first jobs were to list those killed in the pogrom and to conduct a census of the Jewish population still alive. The council was also ordered to establish a Jewish police force, which was to enforce regulations on the movement of Jews inside and outside the city. As hunger among the city's Jews mounted, the Judenrat organized a soup kitchen and provided welfare to the growing numbers of those in need. The next month, it was charged with raising four million rubles. *"The members of the Judenrat went from house to house collecting the money,"* Ephraim wrote, though he added a comment, *"I assume part of it disappeared in their own pockets."*

In the fall of 1941, the Germans began to seize Jews at random, sending them to work camps they had established in the region. Two hundred were abducted in November 1941 and taken to the camp in Lackie Wielkie; over the following weeks, many more Jews were captured and taken to other camps. The Judenrat and families of men sent food and clothes that sometimes arrived and sometimes did not. Many inmates were killed or died from mistreatment, hunger, or epidemics. Though Ephraim's father later died of a heart attack, he was so weakened physically by beatings and torture that Dr. Hreczanik said to Ephraim's mother, *"your husband was killed at the Fortress"* (December 29, 1941).

During the spring of 1942, the Judenrat tried to find employment for Jews in projects of importance to the German economy — the hope was that this work would end random seizures for forced labor. In mid-August, however, the SS ordered the Judenrat to compile a list of three thousand Jews for deportation. The Judenrat members were shocked; most refused to comply and sent out warnings of the impending round up. On August 28th, the Germans launched the ackja (Aktion, in German), which lasted for two days. Many tried to flee or find places to hide — on August 30th, close to 2,700 Jews were seized and deported to the Belzec extermination camp. An entry in his diary the next day began. *"Now we know what an 'akcja' is."*

A little more than two months later, November 2 to 3, the Germans undertook a second akcja — an estimated 2,500 old people, women and children were loaded into trucks and taken to the railway station; there they were herded into freight cars for Belzec. In an extended entry on November 4th, Ephraim wrote, *"Mrs. Reichard knocked on the door screaming, 'they're catching in town!'. . . In the evening the neighbor Glowaski brought news: terrible things are happening in town. The members of the Judenrat were taken as well but not before they took part in the akcja. They collected women, children, and old people. That story crushed us."*

The Nazis set up a small ghetto on December 1, 1942, where they squeezed between 7,500 and 9,000 surviving Jews from Zloczow and nearby communities of Oleski, Sasow, and Bialy Kamien. Many died from starvation and disease. Groups of younger Jews attempted to organize and escape to the forest to join the partisans, though most failed because of the hostility of local Ukrainians.

Hunger in the ghetto was devastating and disease was rampant, including an epidemic of typhus. On April 2, 1943, the Germans liquidated the ghetto. Judenrat head Meiblum was ordered to approve the liquidation — he refused and was murdered on the spot. Two other council members were ordered to sign the approval; they too refused and were murdered. From the market square, the remaining Jews were taken to the village of Jelechowice — there they were killed and buried in pits that had been dug in advance. *"You may well imagine how we received the news,"* Ephraim wrote, in recording Helena's telling about the liquidating akcja of the Jews in the Ghetto, *"[she] told terrible stories. The Jews were loaded on trucks and taken to a clearing in a pine forest near us, beyond the road."* Jelechowice was the same village two-and-a-half miles north of Zloczow where the Ukrainians Hryc Tyz and Misia Koreniuk and Helena Skrzeszewska were hiding Ephraim, his mother and, eventually, thirteen more.

For more than another year, the German army occupied Zloc-zow, always hunting for Jews in hiding. On July 16, 1944, the Soviet army, which had been overrunning other nearby villages and towns, finally entered Zloczow and liberated the city from German occupation — *"THE BOLSHEVIKS HAVE ARRIVED!!!"* the now-16 year old Ephraim wrote. "Three exclamation marks," observed the elder Sten five decades later, "and this phrase is the only one written in red."

Merrill Leffler
Takoma Park, Maryland

Drawings and "inventions" from the diary, 1941-1944

Present-day Ukraine. Until 1939, Zloczow (Zolochiv in Ukrainian) was part of Poland, as was Lvov (L'viv in Ukrainian).

Zloczow, Poland / Tel Aviv, Israel
1941-1944 / 1993-1999

Diary entries from the 1940s are in italics.
Responses from the 1990s are in roman.

People in Zloczow and Jelechowice who appear in Ephraim Sten's diary during the German occupation.

Family
Adolph Sternschuss, father
Anna (née Mann) Sternschuss, mother
Henryk Mann, uncle
Naomi Mann, aunt
Erwin Mann, cousin (their son)

Neighbors and friends of family in Zloczow
Mrs. Reichard
Mrs. Beer
Dr. Schwager
Dr. Hreczanik
Mrs. Lewant

Rescuers in Jelechowice
Hryc Tyz
Misia Koreniuk
Helena Skrzeszewska

Hidden in Jelechowice
Ephraim Sten (née Sternschuss)
Anna Sternschuss
Lipa and Linka Tennenbaum, uncle and aunt
Eda and Selma Tennenbaum, their daughters
Mrs. Edzia Weinstock and Eva Weinstock, her daughter
The Parille family (five)

1941

*Mother knows nothing about Father's murder. I won't be the one to
tell. But I have to express what I'm feeling. I doubt I'll need this
copybook again, so I can use it for a diary. I'll write down all the
details so when I'm old I'll remember my youth and this World
War, even though I'm not sure I'll live through it.*

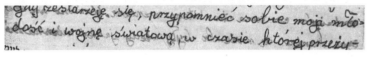

From original Journal in Polish

■ Thus opens my diary. I read what I've just translated and smile.
It's pathetic, this act of translation: a Jewboy keeps a diary during
the Holocaust, the fool somehow is unfortunate enough to survive
— and so the diary has a rather dubious value, particularly when
the outcome is known from the start. Yet I feel that translating it
(from Polish into Hebrew) is like paying a debt. The diary is the
only proof left that I was ever young. So it's my bounden duty not
to change a word, just to leave it as it was when I wrote it more than
fifty years ago.

Maybe merely translating the diary isn't enough. Perspective has
altered, decades have elapsed, but what changed my mind was a
four-day visit to Zloczow. A visit after fifty years. A visit that convinced me that I should exhume the diary from the lower depths of
the bottom drawer of my desk.

And the diary continues.

Today, Friday, July 4, 1941 *— I'm writing while lying on my
back. I can't move my legs. Mother says I'm in shock. Maybe I am.
Maybe I'm so anxious because I can't tell her about Father, who
was drafted yesterday into forced labor and Mother still believes
he's alive.*

■ On the way from the Lvov airport, at the side of the road, I see the sign: Zloczow. Times when I thought I'd invented the place, that it existed only in my imagination.

Now I understand why, when I saw the sign, I changed my mind about the diary. For years, decades, I didn't want to touch it, to dig it out from its natural grave in my desk . . . and suddenly, now, reaching old age. . . .

I look at the letters arranging themselves on the computer monitor while my memory conjures up the sights of Zloczow, and sense that the very act of writing proves that I exist. And even the faint hope that a trace of me will remain.

To paraphrase Descartes: "I scribble, therefore I am."

About six o'clock this morning, I went to Mrs. Schlesinger's to ask if she had any news of my father. As I approached her gate, a German officer emerged and asked where I was going. I replied that a certain professor lived there and I wanted to ask him a question. But the German asked, "Jude?" and of course I said yes, and he drew out his gun to shoot me. I was the fastest runner in my school, but I must have broken a world record as I sprinted away from there.

■ Under our eyelids memories are stored like snapshots. What follows is no exception: a German officer, tall, polished boots, his gun pointed at a big-eared boy in short pants. The boy is running into an alley. On the right, a rough clapboard fence surrounding the post office; on the left, houses; up ahead, the municipal park. And a boy running as if it were just another race at school, but this time the prize is being able to translate this image into words.

And how nice it is now to find the fence still standing, as if remembering my athletic feat.

In streets empty of people but full of military convoys, I ran to Aunt Linka for any news, perhaps through her Ukrainian acquaintances. The gate was locked, so I went to the Brandes' adjoining house and from there I meant to climb over the fence, but in the shadow of the gate I saw a man's body lying on its belly. I couldn't go through, I

*just couldn't. I ran back home gasping, unable to utter a word.
Mother put me to bed, and so I've been lying here for hours. My
mind was blank but suddenly a terrible thought occurred to me:
that the dead man at the gate was my father. He also wore an old
black suit when he was taken away and he too had white hair.*

■ Did I say that memory is like a photo album? Even now, as I'm
translating these sentences, I can still see that image. And during
that visit to Zloczow, when I entered the gate — I suddenly turned
around. On a cobblestone was a dark stain. Could it possibly be
traces of blood from fifty years ago?

*I can write because I'm alone in the house. As soon as it was dusk,
a short time ago, the boards were ripped off the window and two
Germans took Mother to clean an apartment in a nearby house.
When our neighbor, a Ukrainian seamstress, saw them taking
Mother away, she caught up to them so Mother wouldn't be alone.
Scary: darkness, screams from the street, shots. Surely only these
notes will remain.*

■ Isn't it odd that there are so many diaries from this era? Would-
n't it be better if those years vanished in silence? Who needs these
memories? Is it to prolong life, to leave traces, or even to gain
immortality? Or is it to transform raw experience into bricks for a
monument?

*Also, last evening somebody hammered on the boards over the
window. I ran outside to see who it was and saw Mother talking to
two Germans who wanted to know if we had an apartment where
they could sleep. Mother answered yes, saying there was the
apartment left by the Soviets (once it was Father's office) and they
ordered Mother to tidy it up. Of course I helped her and so did
our neighbor, Mrs. Reichard. We put in cushions for a mattress
for them and went back home. That night we didn't sleep.*

■ Today all of us, graduates of TV, know how to shoot a picture.
The hard part in writing is to make the picture clear enough to see

it. Do I have the necessary tools? In addition to the computer, I have to master the language [Hebrew]. And now nothing will help me. This is not my mother tongue, I'm definitely not Conrad — sensitive people will always point to the Polish accent of my writing.

I graduated with straight As, with one exception: Polish. The teacher explained that the highest mark a Jew could possibly earn in Polish is a B. Just as well.

Saturday, July 5th — *Early in the morning, Edzio Kendzierski came and said to Mother: "Don't hope for anything. I was at the Fortress and the ditch where your husband worked was full of bodies." After that, Mother was convinced that Father isn't alive any more. His story affects me in a strange way — I already know it's true. I saw it with my own eyes. But something doesn't make sense. Or perhaps I just can't imagine it.*

■ To what extent I was damaged — that I found out many years later, while visiting Zloczow, coming face to face with landscapes of my youth. Not all the damage was intentional; partly it was because of stupidity or indifference to other people, partly coincidental. And for decades I've been carrying that load on my back and even my grandchildren cannot ease my burden.

Same day, evening, — *Around four o'clock the mother of Mrs. Kitai, Mother's friend, came in and said that Father was alive and staying with them. Hurray! I went wild, jumping, laughing, everything. Mother gave her clean underwear for Father and asked her to tell him to stay there, not to come home, until the situation improved. Mother went out to tell Mrs. Reichard the news, and about an hour later the door opened and Father came in. I'll never forget the sight. His black suit was grey with dirt and dust, on his head he wore some wrinkled hat (belonging to Mrs. Lewant's son; she was afraid of letting Father go without a hat thereby attracting attention to his white hair). He held the package of underwear Mother had sent him and a small army shovel. When he entered I jumped out of bed and screamed, "Mummy!" and ran to him. I* *kissed him although he was terribly stinking, like a corpse — and he started crying. It was the first time I saw Father cry. Together with Mrs. Beer we pulled a sofa into the other room and hid the door behind a mirrored chest. We helped Father remove his clothes and then we saw what the Ukrainians were capable of. His whole back was beaten to a black pulp and swollen and he had a hideous bruise on his head. We washed him and then he ate something and then we put him to bed and he fell asleep. He didn't say a word.*

■ After surviving the war, I decided to bury my memories, to create a life without a past — to go on living. It was better so. It's easier to mingle with normal people living in a free country who don't understand, or don't want to understand, my non-heroic past, to treat me as a soapy stain on their conscience. I know that my very existence disrupts the harmony of life in Zion — please forgive me. If I'd gone up in smoke, it would have been less complicated. So what should I do? Excuse myself for living?

Walking on the streets of Zloczow, I find myself among Ukrainians. There are only Ukrainians. And I keep looking at them as if they were ordinary people, never mind who they were back then. And now? Is their poverty and hunger sufficient punishment?

I'm walking along the streets and everybody is looking at me. Maybe because I look Jewish, maybe because my camera is slung over my shoulder, maybe because of my obviously foreign clothing. I also stop from time to time, pull out a notebook and scribble down something. What does he scribble?

Sunday, July 6th — Our basement is flooded with groundwater. So Father decided to go down there in the morning and stay until evening. I helped him settle in a corner where it's a bit higher and where there's no water. At noon I brought him a meal and he told me what he had gone through. I didn't recognize his monotonous tone, but there, in the darkness of the basement, I sensed that he was reliving his ordeal. Well, in the beginning he worked near the Fortress, burying cadavers of horses. Then he was transferred to the Fortress itself. At the entrance he was ordered to show his papers, but he lied, claiming he had none. "A man is only an addition to his identity card," he said as if he were the father I knew. They worked in two places: the inner court of the prison and the garden. They had to dig up mass graves of corpses killed by the N.K.V.D. [Soviet Security Police]—Ukrainians and Poles (and some Jews like Dr. Grosskopf and his son-in-law). The bodies were laid out in rows to be identified. On that occasion, the Ukrainians beat the Jews, accusing them of committing those murders. Naturally, the Germans and the S.S. troops joined in, beating the Jews mercilessly. Father was followed by a short, white-haired butcher who hit him with a stout stick he had pulled out of the fence, and by a tall, blond S.S. soldier who used a coiled rope. At noon two officers came up to Father and asked his profession. He answered, "Lawyer." Probably they could tell from his accent that he had studied in Vienna, but they asked him anyway. When he confirmed it, one of the Germans asked, "You aren't Jewish, are you?" and Father said he was, and the German, furious, said, "Then I can't do anything for you," and the two of them stormed off. Shortly after, the shooting began. The first to be killed was the well-known madman Herman-Pan. That was his nickname because all the time he repeated, "Poor Herman, Pan Herman [Mr. in Polish]." They went on shooting everybody, except the women, some of whom they even let go. Father saw my friend there, Moniek Spikulitzer.

■ It's too bad my ramblings are not more intelligent. But what can I do? Now, when I've translated this paragraph about the pogrom, I remember the first Israeli Army Independence Day parade that I ever saw. Maybe it seems childish, but I was excited. Before my teary eyes marched a caravan of hazy figures that I had known, a parade that keeps repeating itself every year during the two minutes of the siren's wail in the morning of Holocaust Day. All the figures that have dissolved.

Around three o'clock they shot Father, but as he happened to already be in the ditch, all four bullets hit the pile of dirt, and Father fell down and pretended to be dead. An hour later it started raining and that's what saved him: the Ukrainians and Germans were forced to stop shooting and shelter themselves under the roof.

■ At the Sobieski Fortress, which is going to become a museum, a young curator told me that the bones discovered in the courtyard while the Fortress was reconstructed, were now buried beyond the wall. I went there and had a look.

No tombstone, not even a stone, no sign, nothing.

At 9 p.m. Kuba Schnapp and Freiman pulled Father out of the ditch and all three made their escape. Father practically had to be dragged away because both of them, and two corpses, were lying on his left leg. "After playing Indians," said Father and it seemed to me that he smiled, they slipped through a hole in the fence and parted ways. Father wanted to enter Winczura's house but was refused. He then moved on to Barabasz and there, in the attic, were about thirty people. The next day he was forced to leave because of the terrible conditions. He moved over to a client of his, Mrs. Lewant, and stayed in the attic with the Kitai family. From there he returned home. "One thing is etched in my memory forever," he said, "I never imagined that Jews could die like that. They were like Romans. Proud, erect, silent. Thus they were killed."

■ It doesn't match the stereotype. And that's possibly why survivors are treated with such respect. Maybe that's some solace for the years of terrible humiliation. Once people observe the tattooed number, or hear the magic word "Holocaust," they jump to their feet and give up their seats on the bus, or in the line to buy movie tickets; they are also avid to learn everything about that dark period.

I'm convinced that if those murdered had known how survivors would be treated, they wouldn't have walked — according to Abba Kovner's contemptuous and despicable definition — to their death as sheep led to slaughter, but would have done their utmost to save themselves.

Wednesday, July 9th — *This morning Mother issued a veto and Father didn't go down to the basement. We are sitting in the other room, he's reading a book that looks like a prayer book and I'm writing. He has changed a lot, my Father. Hasn't even asked me what I was writing. He's a different father, not the one who only a few days ago, seeing German soldiers washing themselves at the well in the park for the first time, said, "and thus we returned to Europe." That very same afternoon I saw a car stop not far from the well. Four soldiers got out and shot a passerby.*

■ At night, in a hotel in Zloczow, I had a strange dream. I dreamed I was at the office of the Jewish community in Zloczow and asked its chairman, my father, if we really were in Europe, was he still glad "we returned to Europe." But he turned his back to me and I woke up terribly frightened: somebody touched my arm.

I opened my eyes and found that I was the one sitting in a chair by my bed and stroking my arm. He-I was smiling at me and trying to soothe me with some incomprehensible mumble. I got out of bed and rudely pushed his hand off my arm, and he, the caressing one, vanished into the wall.

I woke up really frightened — for years, so naively, I believed that I corrected Hitler's negligence and finally liquidated the little Jewboy within me: what naiveté.

Mother, who had gone to see what happened to Uncle Henryk, told us about her terrible walk. She had to step over corpses of Soviet soldiers and officers who were killed in street-to-street fighting. She saw a young officer lying on his back, his helmet over his brow, looking as if he were sleeping. Somewhere in Russia his mother was shedding tears over him. During the bombing a porch fell on Uncle Henryk and his head was wounded and bandaged. Father stopped reading and asked me if at least I understood why Bojko, who Father had saved from being deported to Siberia only two months before, now took him to the Fortress and treated him the way he did. I said to Father that I

*didn't know, maybe because he was Ukrainian. And Father said,
"perhaps, perhaps."*

■ I feel very uneasy here, in Zloczow. I walk the streets, remember
all the intersections, all the places, but I don't belong. What has
happened? I jot impressions in my notebook without understanding anything. Why does a person visiting his birthplace fifty years
later not feel any attachment to the place? Do I expect something
marvelous, something that doesn't exist outside of books? Sad, but
it's better so. I'll finish this chapter while I'm still alive, not feeling
any longing, and that's that.

    Is it?

Thursday, July 10th *— A week since "Black Thursday" and it
seems like yesterday: Father was taken about 10 a.m. An evening
earlier Mrs. Reichard came by and told us that at a local Ukrainian meeting, it was decided to carry out an anti-Jewish pogrom the
very next day. Unfortunately, Father didn't believe her because she
was such a gossip. Father was sitting in the kitchen when two
Ukrainians came in, Warwara from our street and Bojko, a tailor
at the Vojentorg [Soviet supply shops for the military]. They told
Father to get ready for work. Father changed into an old suit,
emptied his pockets of everything except a penknife, a handkerchief
and a Soviet I.D. They said to give Father bread because "he would
return only at two in the afternoon and he'd get hungry until
then." (My God, what hypocrisy!) Mother made two sandwiches
with sausage. They also told him to bring a shovel and he kissed
Mother and me and went away. I ran after him to see where they
were taking him. In the park they entered a house where a Post
Office official, Tennenbaum, lived, and then Bojko came out with
Tennenbaum's son, Junek. We also met Milo Schlesinger who told
us his parents had been taken. Another Ukrainian policeman, an
acquaintance of Father's, came by and showed the party card of
Borodaty, Vojentorg's commander who lived in our apartment,
in the rooms that were once Father's office. According to the*

Ukrainian, Borodaty was killed along near Basyliany with all members of the party. Then they took Father and Junek and I went home.

■ At the place where I was separated from my Father on the day of the pogrom, now stands the hotel where I stayed during the four days of my Zloczow stint. Whenever I left the hotel and whenever I came back to it that picture returned to me. My only consolation lies in the fact that despite being new, the hotel is neglected and stinks, and its name is "Ukraine."

At home Mother rushed to prepare a meal for two o'clock. We had a neighbor with us, the widow of a clerk at Bekoniarnia, the local meat-for-export plant, Mrs. Beer with her five-year-old son Jerzy. It was past 11 when Bojko and Warwara again arrived, and Mother being in the courtyard at the very same time they told her to get ready and went on to Mrs. Walltuch. In the meanwhile Mother came into the house to change her stockings and they probably forgot her. . . . In any case, they went away and Mother stayed at home. Mrs. Beer spent all day with us. I settled at the window to watch whether the Ukrainian volunteer policemen would return. I saw only Pniowsky, wearing brown pants, a brown sweater, and a cap with a brown visor, and a blue-and-yellow band round his arm, looking for apartments for soldiers. Two o'clock. There's no Father. Only distant shots are heard from the direction of the Fortress. Four o'clock. Father hasn't arrived. A drizzle was falling and frightened Mother — she sent me to Tennenbaum to enquire if Junek had already returned. A bomb had fallen at their gate and entering there I felt as if a brick was dropping on my head. They hardly opened the door for me — everything was locked up. The moment I came in I saw Junek changing clothes and the whole family crying. When I asked him if he knew what happened to Father, why didn't he return home, maybe something bad happened to him, he replied, "nothing happened to him." Then he corrected himself, "while I was with him nothing bad happened to him." I thanked him, went back and told Mother everything he said. Mrs. Reichard came in. She knew that a pogrom was going on and when Mother told her what Junek said, loud knocks rattled the gate that I left locked for the sake of safety. I went to open it and there was Mrs. Lacher who had a nearby grocery. She came to pick up Dr. Reichard and take him to her sister who had been wounded by shots in the Fortress. I asked her if she saw Father and she answered briefly in Yiddish, "all men were killed." Of course I didn't say anything to Mother and only today told Father how things looked like from here.

■ It reminds me of a story: a short time after arriving in Israel I was taken to a kibbutz in order to get acquainted with that strange entity. There I met an elderly woman who told me she had worked with Janusz Korczak.[1]

For me it was more important that she knew Polish. She showed me the kibbutz which she was — and rightly so — very proud of and derived much pleasure from my amazement. As usual, and without any visible reason, at a certain moment the conversation reverted to the Holocaust.

"You can't imagine how it looked from here," she said, "and how many kibbutz debates we devoted to that subject! You must understand that we held you very close to our hearts." "And what did you do?" I asked. "What do you mean what did we do?" she said, "we worried."

Nice.

They were not alone. Later I learned from Anthony Eden, then Britain's Foreign Secretary — it was screened on TV — that when, sometime toward the end of 1942, he read a statement in Parliament regarding the Holocaust of European Jews, all members of Parliament stood up. Touching, isn't it?

Sunday, July 13th — *I don't know how to define the kind of work I was doing in the morning. It wasn't carpentry despite my sawing and hammering boards and not glaziery despite working on windows. The kitchen is dark. While I was working a truck with soldiers entered the courtyard, drove to the very end and then they*

burst into Dr. Reichard's clinic and threw its whole contents out.
They turned the clinic into a warehouse for good things like candy
or wines to be shipped to the officers at the front. The truck left,
leaving one soldier on guard. His name is Heinz and he used to be
a teacher in Frankfurt. He told me that because I knew German I
would teach him Ukrainian and Russian.

■ More and more I become convinced that I had written this diary
for myself, a kind of confession, but now — how weird! — I don't
have any objection to other people reading those papers. Schopen-
hauer wrote in his time that ordinary, simple people, if they have
the right components, can create important, inspired books. I
would add, particularly with the unbearable lightness of the computer.

Georges Sand wrote somewhere that writing a diary signifies
that the author had stopped thinking of the future and decided to
totally live in the past. I wouldn't say that it was completely true . . .

Tuesday, July 15th — *Today we went with Heinz to the barracks*
to pick up pickled cabbage. Some Ukrainian fellow attacked me
and Heinz kicked him in the belly. He has thick, short boots. The
Ukrainian cringed and ran away crying. We found Soviet military
maps of our whole area there. Tonight I'll paste them into one big
map.

■ I walk along the streets of Zloczow and the places mentioned in
my diary come to life. As if I had written a travel guide in those
days. Here's the barracks that always remind one of a memory picture of the kind preserved behind the eyelids. The distribution of
pickled cabbage and the madding crowd. As a matter of fact it was
a continuation of the regular behavior in the no man's land
between the outgoing and incoming regimes. Always the same,
repetitive and threatening picture: the rabble attacking shops and
breaking shop windows with the backdrop of dull shouts, curses,
loud groans and boots creaking on glass smithereens. Peasants

from the neighborhood, unfamiliar faces with burning eyes, looting whatever they can get hold of. With their crooked fingers they drag off clothes and kitchen accessories, towels and drapery, shirts, shoes, bed sheets and of course an incredible quantity of alcohol. Rushing off to deposit their spoils and returning for another round of pillage. On such occasions the mob is really frightening. Isaac Babel had already recorded that in his "Dovecot," and other writers too — after all, our people have had their history of pogroms.

And how strange it is that today, writing about that, the streets of Zloczow are always etched in my memory along with the unbridled rabble. Why don't we remember other pictures?

Friday, July 18th — This morning a frightened Mrs. Reichard arrived and told us German soldiers were robbing Jews. At once Heinz picked up his rifle and settled down at the gate. He said he would kill any robbing soldier on the spot because "a soldier is forbidden to rob, it's not right for a soldier to do that." Nobody came to us. Perhaps they saw Heinz and were afraid, or it was just a gang that arrived and then left.

■ No gate. No house. Nothing has remained. A monument of Pushkin sprouted in our courtyard instead of a lilac bush. Surely Heinz must have vanished too. How odd it is but he's the only German, among all those I ran into, that the diary mentions positively. Blond, faded, thin, a bit bent and a bit sad. I doubt he found his place in the other, new Germany. That Germany where a newspaper headline declared: "Killing Jews by gas is a victory of economic principles, says a senior German officer." Of course

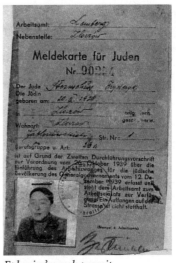

Ephraim's work permit

he's right, just think of the price of millions of bullets . . . And how happy it makes one, the fact that there's something stable left in the changing world.

Thursday, August 14th — *Heinz and the chocolates left a week ago. They moved closer to the Front. We said farewell to each other and who knows if he's still alive. A couple of days ago they declared that all Jews from 13 to 60 years old must work. I began working as an errand boy at the Judenrat.[2] I work there every day. To be more precise, I run all the time. For this I receive a quarter of a black bread loaf, but after all the running I feel so hungry that I consume my portion in one gulp. And that's a big bread, two kilos!*

■ At the hotel's restaurant, sitting down for the first dinner, the waitress asked me what I wanted to order. What a question! For years I dreamed of Ukrainian borsht. Regrettably we don't have it today, the waitress said, but tomorrow it will be all yours. The next day, when she asked the same question, I replied that I already had ordered it the night before. The embarrassed waitress explained they just didn't have it, it was impossible to get the beets. No beets in Ukraine! It's like being told that the sand ran out in the Sahara.

Thursday, August 21st — *In the morning I had a bellyache and didn't go to work. Before noon a truck arrived. Two Germans got out. One who looked like an officer pointed at the piano and asked who played it. Mother, with her usual pride, said it was me and that experts predicted I had a bright future as a pianist. The German smiled and asked me to play. I played the "Elfentanz," which I recently performed in the concert at the end of the school year at the conservatory. The Germans stood, listened and when I finished the officer said, "very nice, very nice," signaled the other who then went out and returned with several soldiers. They took the piano, loaded it on the truck and drove away. Mother didn't even cry. There's more space in the room now.*

■ That officer was probably a music critic in his civilian life.

September 16th — The bread ration has been reduced to 1.50 kg and it's not worthwhile to work any longer. Father works for The Mutual Help of the Jewish community in Zloczow. That's good because as a manager he has received a formal card from the Judenrat. Dr. Meiblum[3] asked Father to join the Judenrat but he turned it down.

■ That's the reason my father didn't work at the Judenrat office. His office was on Mickiewicz Street, a street drawn by two lines of trees. Not an avenue but spots of green. The street began at a bookstore where every week I used to buy the Tom Mix and Buffalo Bill magazines. Adjoining it was a pharmacy, and then a few houses and a small hotel for traveling agents, and opposite it was a restaurant where we used to eat whenever the painters took possession of the house. A friend of my mother's lived on that street and often we would visit her or a schoolmate of my father's. Now there's neither a hotel nor a restaurant, the friends have disappeared and even the trees found their way to the furnace. I loved Mickiewicz Street. It ended at the entrance to the market, at the very place where a German tried to kill me.

Monday, September 25th — The Germans demanded — and received from the Judenrat— a one-time levy, incredibly high.[4] The members of the Judenrat went from house to house collecting the money. I assume part of it disappeared into their own pockets. Dr. Schwager has been living with us for more than a month. His wife doesn't stop crying, days and nights, over Uri, their murdered son. Only Mother has a positive influence over her. I'm forbidden to approach her, even show myself. Uri was a friend of mine. Mother is afraid that I'd remind his mother of her son.

■ Uri — when he was a child he called himself Uli, and the name stuck — was handsome, dark and stronger than all of us. I envied his success with the girls. Like us he recoiled from all those anti-Semitic digs but he never talked, he used his fists. The beaten fellows patiently waited and the day after the German arrival they lured him from the house under some pretext, took him to the fields out of town and there they slaughtered him.

While translating my diary into Hebrew I started having a strange sensation: the figures appearing in it resemble a radio play — they exist only when they act and immediately disappear. In most cases they disappear in the ambivalent sense of the term. How big is the cemetery inhabiting my memory!

Friday, November 11th — This morning a cousin of mine was born. They called him Erwin. Aunt Naomi and Uncle Henryk waited eleven years for that child. Is this the right time to raise children? There's war, there are Germans. . . . . I'll have a brother that I didn't have before.

■ Nothing has remained of Erwin. Not even one faded photo. Maybe one grain of a statistic.

When my first grandson was born I was surprised to discover that in my mind, time and again, I called him Erwin though his name is Nimrod.

Tuesday, December 23rd —We are observing the Shiv'ah[5]. I don't know if there's anything more awful. People keep coming all the time and won't let us be alone for even one moment. In the morning and in the evening we need a minyan,[6] but multitudes arrive. Everything began on the last Sabbath. As usual we had lots of guests. Dr. Schwager, the Wartenbergs, Dr. Reichard with Edzio, Klarr with his daughter, Mrs. Beer with Jerzy, Dr. Teichmann. They talked, analyzed the political situation, prophesized a near end to the war. Father was in an excellent mood, laughed, joked. When everybody went away, he planned to have an office without any staff, only hire a good cook and Mother would help him in the office. We went to bed. About 9 o'clock I woke up because of Father's moans. I woke Mother, switched the light on and then realized that Father was having a heart attack. We hurriedly put on our clothes and Mother started to heat water on the primus for compresses. When nothing seemed to help I ran to Dr. Reichard.

He came, gave Father a shot, checked his pulse and went back to bed. Father relaxed a bit, but after a short time began to moan and his breathing became wheezy. Again I rushed to bring Dr. Reichard who came and said Father caught a cold from the compresses. Again he checked his pulse and departed. The scene was repeated twice. In the morning Father had a terrible attack. I ran to bring Dr. Hreczanik but he wasn't at home. I therefore alerted Dr. Gerber. On the way I stopped at Aunt Linka's to report to her. We hurried home and on the way, by the Judenrat, we met Dr. Hreczanik. He came along with us and the three doctors, including Dr. Reichard, began trying to save Father. They took blood, gave him shots and father improved considerably. He opened his eyes and seeing the three doctors said, "if all of you are here, I am surely dying." The kitchen was full of people. Everybody who could manage, came to ask after father's health. All talked about the statement made by the Governor General Dr. Frank who spoke on the radio about the need to help the soldiers and give them furs. The doctors went away, and Father was quiet all day. In the afternoon all the regular members of the "Club" assembled but Mother wouldn't let them go in to Father and they managed the world in the kitchen. She let them only peep in for a moment. Dr. Hreczanik came, talked to Father, soothed him and went away. Dr. Schwager offered to sleep in our house but finally we remained on our own. We went to bed in our clothes. I woke up because of Father's heavy breathing. His condition deteriorated. I ran to Dr. Reichard, he gave him another shot, sat down a bit and then left. An hour, or an hour and a half later, again Father worsened. Again I ran to Dr. Reichard, knocked on his door with all my strength and implored him to hurry. I heard Mother screaming "Adzio!" and Mrs. Reichard said to her husband, "it's a waste of time," but he came, gave Father a shot. Father opened his eyes, looked at me and died. It was five a.m. Father lay on his back, his mouth slightly open, seemingly asleep. I don't know how time passed until seven when Linka came to ask about Father. Then Uncle Henryk arrived, acquaintances, friends. At two in the afternoon they came to wash Father and then the funeral started on its way. Everything was hazy with me and I don't remember much. Only that we came back without Father.

■ The funeral went past the barracks across from the street corner, went quickly, probably in order to avoid the Germans. Went quickly but not at a marching pace, but impelled by some inner impulse to get it done, and the sooner the better.

Indeed, my vision became foggy because tears filled my eyes. There, at my father's funeral I decided not to weep any more. Never. Only thus will I regain the sharpness of sight.

Monday, December 29th — *Today we finished the Shiv'ah. We went to Father's grave. We cried. After that Black Thursday Mother said, "You haven't anyone any longer to bid him good night, daddy." And she's right. Only those who have lost their fathers will understand me — and regrettably there are so many now. Dr. Hreczanik was right when he said to Mother, "your husband was killed at the Fortress." Father definitely returned from there a different man. Despite his death I'll go on consulting him on anything. My father is a wise man and knows everything.*

■ At the entrance to Zloczow — from the west, the direction of Lvov — was the Jewish cemetery. More than a hundred years ago, when the Austrians decided to pave a road, they demanded the Jews should evacuate the cemetery that clashed with the planned route. The frightened Jews had only one solution — to pray. And it helped: on the very last night before the paving of the cemetery began, it split into two parts. Since then the right part is called "old" and the left part "new."

Today it's difficult to see the two because numbers of garages have been built on the right side, and in the new cemetery not even one tombstone is left. Not even one protrusion suggesting a grave. Everything is pressed down, smoothed. I couldn't recite the Kaddish[7] over my father's grave.

1942

January 19th — *Twice a day I go to recite the Kaddish at the "shtibel" opposite Dr. Gruber's. It's not so pleasant in the morning: dark, cold. On the way I pick up the dentist Braun and his son. I prefer walking with them.*

■ Even now, more than fifty years after arriving in Israel, every evening on the second day of Tevet, I go to the synagogue to recite the Kaddish. Now I can read and even understand the prayers even if I don't understand what I'm doing there, mumbling, a lonely non-believer with a skullcap on his head. Once a year the tradition immersed in the blood wakes up, completely ignoring my secularity. It's not a charade, no lie whatsoever, maybe an expression of memory or a homage.

Or maybe I go to the synagogue because I know my father would have wanted that.

I don't work at the Judenrat anymore. The work there is both hard and not worth it financially. So Aunt Linka arranged for me to have a fictitious card testifying to the fact that I'm a laborer in military construction. It's a sham because I've never set foot there; I don't even know where the site is. I take advantage of my spare time to — among other things — visit Erwin who was very sick and even went through surgery. He had an abscess on his chest, like his mother. Now he's back at home and getting better. A beautiful, cute baby.

■ It seems to me — if I'm not wrong — that in that time we were ordered to wear a white armband with a blue Star of David. It's odd that such an important event, so typical to the beginning of the Era of Humiliation, was not mentioned in the Diary. It wasn't recorded either how we tried to hide the armband by nonchalantly carrying the coat over the arm. It also wasn't recorded how the religious men suddenly began to suffer from toothaches and went about hiding their beards under a rag.

February 14th — Most of the time I spend with Celek Kiewtz and Edzio Klarr. We have a trench in the garden left by the anti-aircraft defense. Celek brought a Fiat grill. We put it over our trench, covered it with branches and leaves and one cannot see anything

Armband Jews had to wear

even from one meter away. We have a place to sit in and think up plans. We started with "taking care" of the Soldatenheim [Soldier's home]. It seems very simple: from the corner of our basement we'll dig up to the corner of the Soldatenheim, which is only a matter of crossing the street. I said it wouldn't work because we need to fortify it all with a sewer pipe, one of those big ones in which it's possible to walk. Celek thinks we can dig only in depth, not from above. Probably, but where can we get such a huge concrete pipe? And then, in the nights, we'll steal into the house, butcher some Germans and that's that. I said that my father told me how they had managed to overcome a plague of rats when he served as a commander of an Italian prisoners' camp in the last war. They caught a big rat, cut out its eyes and hanged a little bell round its neck. The rat went mad, ran out of the camp and the rest of the rats followed it. If we could train rats to gobble up the Germans after the slaughter — we wouldn't leave traces. Like King Popiel[8] and the rats of Lake Goplo, said Edzio. The Germans will panic, bring soldiers, and surround the Soldatenheim with a joint chain carrying Schmeisers [German submachine gun] — to no avail. We always can enter through the tunnel, wreak havoc on them and send rats to cover our tracks. We sat a long time in our trench and worked out the plan to the minutest detail.

■ I stood by house no. 22 on Ujeski Street, the house I was born in. I was standing there thinking whether it was a good idea to bring my children over here, a kind of roots searching expedition that is so fashionable now. Are they genuine roots? Or perhaps damaged ones? My life has been a denial of Zloczow, consciously or subconsciously. And there is no doubt that my children's roots are in Tel Aviv. So what do they have to do with Zloczow? Is that a nostalgic return, an outcome of age? Is it desirable to pass my hump of the past on to them?

True, I did have a happy childhood, as was to be expected for being an only child. But five years smashed the happiness to smithereens.

April 25th — For almost a month I've been working as a storeman at "Old Products and Leftovers," a nice name for junk. Here I really have to work and by now I can distinguish, even in the dark, between cast and forged iron. We transfer the goods to the train, they are loaded on the cars and then sent away to be processed at steel plants. Uncle Henryk got me that job — he works there as an accountant. This kind of work is considered safe and protected because the whole business belongs to Goering.

■ A picture from memory: I'm driving in a truck, sitting on the iron pile, on the way to the train platform where the cars are waiting to be loaded.

As it seems now, nobody has swept or tidied up the platform where I had worked. Maybe it's possible to find the leftovers here. Maybe even the remnants of furniture the Jews had lost on the very same platform when they were loaded on the cars on their way to Belzec.

Metallic badge of forced labor

*Sunday, May 4th — A completely crazy week has just ended.
Finally my Uncle returned home. He had spent a week at the
Lackie camp.*[9] *It's so good Mother managed to free him. Thank
God. No matter how much it cost, what's important is that he's
home. Everything began in a stupid way. Uncle went to work and
already near the office he ran into Warzog who was riding his white
horse to the camp. Warzog stopped and ordered my uncle to identify himself. Uncle gave him the papers and Warzog, from high on
the horse, asked, "Are you Mann? Heinrich Mann?" Uncle didn't
understand and said "certainly." "If so," said Warzog, "I'm taking
you to the camp so that everybody will see that I have a Kreisleiter
[District commissioner] with me in the camp." He ordered Uncle
to walk by the horse. Probably he meant it as a German style joke.
It truly is a strange coincidence and maybe unfortunate as well
that the Kreisleiter's name is Heinrich Mann [The German writer,
Thomas Mann's brother]. I saw him once when the Judenrat
bought Father's office for him. He's tall and fat and wears a
uniform, not thin like Uncle. But the name is truly identical,
although there's no family connection between us, that's for sure.*

■ In that time I was ignorant of another Heinrich Mann. Somewhat more famous than my uncle and even than the Kreisleiter.
Certainly Warzog didn't know of him either.

*When Mother learned of that she ran to Weinstock at the Judenrat
and asked him to set Uncle free. She promised him gold and
indeed, two days later he came and told her how much Warzog
demanded. I think a respectable portion of those "demands" found
its way to Weinstock's pocket. Did we have an alternative? He's the
only "macher" who can approach Warzog. Mother gave him what
he asked for but Warzog didn't release Uncle immediately. First he
had to show off his own Kreisleiter to all his German acquaintances. Finally he let Uncle go, a little thinner, a little more tired.
Aunt Naomi says that Erwin recognized him and was very happy.
We always knew he was a very smart baby. Only let's hope that
Warzog won't demonstrate his sense of humor again.*

■ Reading this morning's newspaper I was beset by a feeling of déjà vu, as if I had already read it. Again some tyrant in the neighborhood would like to annihilate us and the world is amazed at our lack of flexibility. Again a natural catastrophe in the sub-continent. Again a minister parading his stupidity. Again a returning tourist discovered anti-Semitism in Poland. But there was a surprise for me as well: a news item copied from some French newspaper reveals that my "acquaintance" Obersturmbahnführer Franz Warzog has been living somewhere in Syria under the name Achmed Larui. Living peacefully and contentedly, because this is one of the very few places in the world where he doesn't expect Jews to come and settle accounts with him. At least in the next war, that surely is bound to happen, there is a chance a bomb will drop on his villa.... Enough of that.

Thursday, June 5th — *I've been promoted. I've become a sammler. I collect. Mother, too, does collecting. But she doesn't show up for work. I collect for the two of us. We don't have money to buy with, so I have to collect and I have to supply two quotas, that is 3,600 kgs of iron per month. I established a partnership with the sister of my girlfriend Lena, Fela Friedmann, and her mother. I found some iron in the warehouses of the coal mines, about 20 tons. That will do for two months. I also found hundreds of bottles at my friend Munek Seidenbaum's. So we manage.*

■ Probably an earthquake visited Zloczow. Its streets have become shorter, the houses lower, everything has shrunk. But that doesn't impede memories at every corner, at every step. Here lived a friend of mine, Seidenbaum, there was Lerner's barbershop, and over there the dentist Braun.

Monday, July 10th — *It's good that this diary exists. I always used to tell Mother and Father everything. But there are a growing number of happenings that shouldn't be told in the first place. At least one can unburden oneself on paper. It helps like ersatz [substitute]. Still, it's something.... In the afternoon I went to Rysiek to exchange a book. He accompanied me on the way back. In the Green Market Murdi the gendarme caught us and ordered us to walk with him. He was royally drunk and led us to the other side of the market, to the ruins of a house that was already bombed at the beginning of the war. There he drew a gun and told Rysiek to stand by the wall so that he could shoot him. Rysiek refused. Murdi, who could hardly stand on his feet, began shouting, waving his gun about and pleading with Rysiek to do him a favor and obey him. But Rysiek was stubborn. I wanted to tell Murdi to let us go but he screamed at me to keep quiet and wait patiently until he killed Rysiek and then he would take care of me. The discussion went on and on till Rysiek couldn't take it any longer, told Murdi that he was pressed for time and maybe some other time, and that we had to go. We sprinted among the houses taking passages known only to us. Murdi ran after us shooting crazily and then lost us, or maybe we lost him. In any case, he missed and didn't harm us. It's a fact: I can write this whole story.*

■ Some years later, Rysiek died in Warsaw of a sudden, unexpected, heart attack.

Which proves to what extent the Holocaust disease resembles radiation. One can never tell when it will show up, when its viruses will attack.

Like returning to this diary years later.

August 31st — Now we know what "akcja" is. We heard of it earlier but didn't comprehend it. Now we do. Three days ago, on the 28th, in the afternoon, there was a terrible panic. Because we had arranged with Hryc to preserve a hideout for us I pressed Mother to go there. Hryc himself came around four o'clock and wanted to take me along with Celek. But Celek adamantly refused. So I didn't go either (who knows, if we did go, might his mother be alive?) The town was mourning. We went to sleep at the Wartenbergs in order not to stay alone. There they have an excellent hideout where we can hide if need be. We sat together till late at night and then went to bed in our clothes. At six in the morning Wartenberg got up and

went out to work but immediately came back in panic: "Quick!
They are here!" At that very moment a "schupo"[10] and other
Germans with the Jewish policeman Schapira came in.

■ Question: Would the Germans be able to guess that in this house,
in a purely Polish neighborhood, there were Jews without the kind
help of Mr. Schapira from the Ordnungdinst [the accessory police
force]?

It was too late to escape. One German came directly to us and
demanded to see our work papers. Last evening I closed the pocket
with a safety pin, I was excited and by the time I managed to open
the pocket he wanted to take me along. Finally I showed him the
papers and he let me be. In the meanwhile Schapira said that he
was pulled out of bed at 2 a.m., the Gestapo and "flying Schupo"
arrived from Tarnopol. The situation in town is terrible. Everybody
is taken. When they finished checking the papers they found that
Celek did not have any document because he was too young. So
they decided to take him. Celek went to his mother to bid her
farewell and the sight touched the black haired Gestapo man's
heart. He said he couldn't part them and therefore took the mother
as well. Then they left. For a passing moment we moved around,
shocked. Wartenberg went to his work at the Gendarmerie, Kiwetz
ran to the Judenrat to look for help and we entered the hideout in
the attic in the courtyard. I didn't stay there for a long time but got
out and stood on guard. If the Germans returned I had to warn the
people hiding and escape to the gardens. At noon the Germans
arrived to eat at the Soldatenheim and among them I recognized
one that came to us in the morning. In the afternoon, when I
returned to the hideout, Kiwetz came too, crying and cursing —
cursing the Judenrat and everybody else. Before the fall of evening
Mrs. Lewek burst in, happy at the return of Celek. Kiwetz went out
and somewhat later came back with Celek, all washed clean and
shiny. Celek told us that earlier all of them were assembled near the
Judenrat and there he could make his escape but didn't want to
leave his mother. Later they were transferred in a truck to the train

depot and immediately crammed into the cars. His mother and he preferred waiting on the side. They waited there for several hours. Celek tried to escape but to no avail. Finally he took off his shoes, hung them on a stick that he held over his shoulder, bid farewell to his mother and marched out the main gate without any trouble. The German standing there looked at him and said nothing. At the station some kids from the neighborhood pounced on him but he explained to them that he was no Jew and was just taking care of a herd of cows near the depot. They let him be.

■ Celek: a boy looking like a pure sheygets, no Jewish characteristics whatsoever, an upturned nose, blue eyes, fair hair — perfect. A few months later, with forged papers, he moved with his father to Lvov and there roamed the streets as a newspaper boy. He was so successful that he forgot who he really was, went down to a public urinal, and there somebody saw him pissing and noticed his penis. Thus was Celek murdered.

Mother asked him if he saw anybody familiar. Celek said, "At the train station were your brother, his wife and his son." It was as if a lightning hit us. Mother said, "I felt . . . ." Erwin didn't live even one year.

■ In the morning, when the Germans still acknowledged papers and deluded themselves that they could fulfill the quota with unemployed people, they arrived at Uncle Henryk's house. They released Aunt Naomi because she had the right kind of papers (they were forged) but announced they had to take the baby, Erwin. Of course she went with the baby in her arms. Uncle Henryk saw them being taken away out the window of his protected office, went out and joined them on the way to the train station. Near the cars the Obersturmbahnführer Warzog, who wanted to release him, or rather to install him again as a curiosity in his own camp, discovered him. He was even prepared to release Henryk's wife as well but refused to hear about letting the baby go. He couldn't understand why they insisted on turning down his offer to be released but to leave the baby behind. So the three of them went on the train.

Thus only the Mann Auditorium in Tel Aviv remains of the Mann family, and to the best of my knowledge Frederick Mann had nothing to do with my mother's family.

Yesterday, before nightfall, we emerged from our hiding place and returned home. The door was broken and the house was turned upside down. The Gestapo went away, the trains with their cargo went away, and the akcja was over.

■ Stanislaw Lec[11] wrote in his *Unkempt Thoughts* that "whoever goes through tragedy is not necessarily a tragic hero." I remember that when I read the final pages of the translated diary.

Monday, September 1st — *This morning began with an akcja of apartments. A German with a name of Mock, better known as schmuck, is in charge. In the morning Mother went to the office to pick up notices to stick on the door in order to prevent the furniture from being taken away. I locked the apartment and sat outside and then they showed up. Weinstock (who directed the akcja on behalf of the Judenrat) asked me who was working for us and why the notice on the door did not elaborate on that. I explained to him that both of us were employed and the notices were on the way. He mumbled something and went on to the Reichards. I decided to escape to the gardens. On the way I ran into Schultze of the Sonderdienst. He hit me viciously with a steel ruler on the back and I could hardly breathe.*

■ It was like receiving a degree from the representative of the super-race, the abusing people awarding a kind of title to the representative of the abused. The Germans, despite history, the defeats, will always belong to the abusing nations. This is the reason why they could afford paying reparations to those who managed to survive them. They fixed an exact rate of payment, something that goes along with the German national character. On that list they marked the price of a mother, a father, a grandfather, a child according to his or her age. One may grow rich, if only one remembers who are the main beneficiaries.

At the beginning of 1945, after the liberation of Auschwitz, Ilya Ehrenburg[12] visited there and later wrote that in order to finally solve the problem of peace in Europe one has to activate the machinery of extermination and put all Germans into it. Ehrenburg was right but Alexandrov, the party's propagandist, published a scathing article against Ehrenburg in *Pravda*. Even Stalin lost his cool and commented that "Hitlers come and go but the German people remain forever." No doubt about that.

Despite that grievous beating I managed to cross over Kendzierski's courtyard and through to Kociubinski's garden. From there I saw Mock with his dog, a truck entering the courtyard and finally, Mother coming back. I got out of the thicket and returned too. The notices had already been put on the door and I found that I saved the whole apartment because by the time they were going to break the door open, Mother returned and proved to them we were working and so we were saved being sent along with the rest.

■ I doubt very much whether we had any notion what those transports really meant. We definitely didn't know that it was a one-way trip.

Whenever I stop translating from the original Polish in order to type a comment I find myself thinking about whether the need to comment is the reason for my stopping the translation and if those comments of mine are direct or indirect associations deriving from the diary? Or maybe my visit in Zloczow was a kind of catalyst?

For years I dreamt of going there and xeroxing the pictures of my memory with my camera (why not? Weegee[13] too came from Zloczow). The dream has been realized but maybe it would have been better to avoid the confrontation and to leave only the idealizing memories.

I don't belong to the happy ones. The happy ones have a weak memory and plenty of fantasies.

Tuesday, September 2nd — *How fortunate it is that Mother has so many friends among the railway workers. She sent one of them to Rawa Ruska because the cars had delivery notices with that address. She thinks my uncle is probably to be found in that camp.*

■ Illusions, illusions. . . . But who knew that Rawa Ruska was a crossroads on the way to Belzec? Or who knew what Belzec[14] meant with the exception of the well-known Yiddish song?

Grandfather Franz, Mother's father, was the director of the railway station. Uncle Henryk had been left with an encyclopedia of trains, five big beautiful volumes. I used one of them in the first grade when I played the role of an imp and recited, "It's a book from heaven in which all words are given"! The book was heavy and when I bent down to pick it up, my pants, made of blue construction paper, burst open. A good source for developing stage fright. . . .

I remember this because I wanted to mention that my mother's family belonged to the railway workers. All of them lived by the station. One uncle was a cashier, another was in charge of cargo, and yet another ran a restaurant at the depot. All of them derived their livelihood from the railway and of course my childhood memories were full of the smell of locomotive smoke. There also were lots of Polish friends or acquaintances from among the railroad employees. Once upon a time, they were like a family, but when the Germans arrived they just vanished from the face of the earth.

Maybe the uncles were better than the neighbors, even if they were not more affluent, in caring for their families, the education of the children, the future (really!), possibly. Was this the reason for the envy that became so prominent after the decimation of the family, the kind of envy that gave birth to "in any case everything will be lost or taken over by the Germans — isn't it better that we, the relatives, the historical neighbors, inherit it?"

The percentage of Polish collaborators with the Germans was minute; I think it was the same as the percentage of people who helped the Jews. The overwhelming majority of Poles was simply indifferent. They could not liquidate the Jews with their own hands. Oh, not that way. But they had no objection to the job being perpetrated by the Germans whom they hated or the Ukrainians whom they despised: Let *them* do it and relieve us of "the problem." That is why the overwhelming majority did not lift a finger to help. The Jews didn't have any possibility of surviving in the hostile ocean surrounding them. And if one could also gain something under the circumstances. . . .

Poland was the perfect center for the Jewish liquidation.

We took a few clothes from Uncle Henryk's apartment to serve his needs when he comes back. I doubt we can save the apartment, despite the fact that Mother managed to settle a Polish woman, an acquaintance of ours, Marysia Tarnawska, so that she could keep her eye on the contents.

■ Household items — as in the paintings of Yossel Bergner,[15] or in the poem by Wladyslaw Szlengel[16] — have a life of their own, but grow weaker when moved from place to place, and each time they grow fewer.

As an author of an autobiography I thought my stories would be of interest to everybody, despite the fact that they interest only me. Somehow I forgot that other people have their own autobiographical stories and they think that only those stories are of any interest.

Maybe it will become different when we, all the survivors of that era, croak, the numbers on the arms will grow faint till they are faded away, the ruins of the camps will completely disintegrate, and finally everybody will love everybody.

Wednesday, September 10th —*Yesterday I went to Jelechowice, to Hryc. I came there with Fela Friedmann, my partner. Hryc said he had old iron in his possession and indeed we found about 200 kilograms. I was very well received there, drank sour milk and also fresh and sweet. In the evening an acquaintance of ours arrived, a forester by the name of Parille. We told him the news he was ignorant of because he spends all his time in the village. The night was terrible. I was eaten alive by fleas or lice.*

■ Shall I confess? In spite of the hateful vermin it was the first time I slept with a woman. And also one who was older than me, married and experienced. . . . I don't like to write about that, but I have to admit that I then discovered, the first time in my life, that at the height of the experience, the ears become plugged and one hears the first six notes of "Ave Maria."

Since then I have known for sure how and when Schubert composed that piece of music.

Which did not impede those many bites.

In the morning, I got up angry at the whole world. I went to the head of the village, got a wagon from him, loaded the iron and we drove back to town. After depositing it all in the warehouse I was informed of a telephone call from the center in Zborow and that I was to return again to my old job as a "collector." I am happy that I'll have one quota less, but I'm busy all day and it's so difficult under such circumstances to collect iron for Mother as well.

I've been working all my life. As early as the beginning of that forced labor. I've never been idle and have always done my duty. I don't think it's only because of the wages — definitely not. It also is a matter of character and doing my social duty. Now I've become a burden on society because it allegedly repays the debt in paying my pension. And that's that. But if I suddenly croak, it would be of no interest to anyone. Only one thing will be considered: my humble contribution to public thrift.

Were the Eskimos right? But where are our icy wastes and polar bears?

Monday, September 15th — *Yesterday I got a day off. In the morning we went with Fela Friedmann to Polipce. There was lots of iron there, but the head of the village was drunk, refused to give us a wagon and so we returned with empty hands.*

■ Somebody is playing Chopin's "Étude in E Minor." It's on the radio, by the way. The sounds of the piano fill the room, the heart.

The diary is supposed to remind one of that cliché about the phoenix rising from its ashes. What becomes clearer and clearer in this writing is that the ashes are the end. And that's that. The writing was supposed to be a contribution to memory, recycling a dark period in life, but in retrospect I'm convinced it was born by mistake. The pianist on the radio has progressed to the "Mazurka in A Minor." Innocently I thought that writing would be fun, an occupation for a retiree. An intentional disposal of too much free time. And also an intriguing meeting with myself as I was more than fifty years ago. But one has to pay for everything, and in this case, the price is too much. It's a debt that I pay in my old age. For decades I was not conscious of the load crushing my soul. This damned writing has newly rediscovered everything.

Thursday, September 18th — *Germans love dogs. It seems to me that every officer walks around with a scary dog. Mock, who lives by our house, the one who is in charge of military provisions, has a big German shepherd that always keeps as close as possible to his master's legs. But the biggest dog of all belongs to Witlitzky. This is a spotted great Dane, as big as a calf. Witlitzky doesn't move without it. When his car stops the dog gets out first and only afterwards Witlitzky. They constantly make rounds among the ruined houses. Witlitzky's Jews dismantle the ruins and later clean the bricks with knives. Then they load the bricks on trucks, and later reload the same bricks on train cars and all of that is sent to build the Atlantic Wall.[17] I can only hope that the dispatched loads include the original fleas from Zloczow. When Witlitzky beats someone, his dog bites him as well. How lucky that I don't work there. Rysiek says that the Germans are attached to dogs not in order to frighten someone else but because they are scared themselves. Scared of whom?*

■ Many people do not understand that all of us went through a cold blooded, planned process of dehumanization. Like that band around the arm, the details were little and seemingly unimportant. Like the edict forbidding walking on sidewalks, the order to take the hat off when meeting Germans, gradual starvation — finally, death became salvation.

The murdered ones were not saints, but persecuted, tortured.

Friday, September 19th — *Today was a good day. After work I found more than 800 kgs of iron and copper near the hospital. I saved Mother's quota. And besides, the partnership with Fela broke up. They have two quotas and though I am only one, they wanted to divide it into two thirds and a third. But only Fela and I collect. So I demanded a fifty-fifty division. They refused and now each one is on his own. A pity.*

■ Always odd and freshly amazing. All those people who are indebted to me for doing something for them, a doing that sometimes became a career, are unable to forgive me and feel well when not noticing my absence. Those people who once were so glad to see me . . .

Sunday, September 21st — *We had a visit by Mrs. Skrzeszewska, Helena. We were very glad. She came from Belzec, where her husband Karol serves in the Polish police. As usual she was full of pep, could not sit still even for one moment, and was in constant motion. She suggested to Mother that we should go back with her and that Mother could work as a housekeeper for a forester not far from Belzec. The only problem was how to get me over there because the Germans can take my pants off. Helena cares very much about what happens to me. She has no children and she has been my friend since before the war, when we spent one summer with them. I enjoyed it there. Her house stands by a big forest. You can stretch your hand out the window and touch the trees. Not far from there is a lake and everything is so peaceful.*

■ When I look today from the top of my old age at the road that led to it, I see the mistakes I made. Once they said that I was "naïve." Naïve? No, just stupid! A child can be naïve. Maybe a youngster, but later? It's so sad that one has gained one's bit of common sense only now, and only now understands the past. Sabato[18] wrote something similar, but he is entitled to write like that: he is Sabato.

I remembered that peacefulness when I went to Hryc's two weeks ago. He worked for years for Skrzeszewska and now he guards their house and the farm. Misia Koreniuk, a teacher from Zazule, who was Karol's lover before the war, lives with him. Karol was the chief of the police in Zloczow and when the Soviets arrived, he hid with us for a few days and then escaped across the San to the German side. When I visited them he put me on a horse, taught me how to take care of beehives, was very nice.

■ No. The general tone of the diary, the hopeless shuffle though the grayish daily life is driving me nuts. It's no wonder that I remembered a schoolmate, Henjo-Schmuck. It's not nice to address a friend that way, but that's what I recollected from our youth. Now he is a celebrated physician. So I went to him and said, "Henjo, I don't need to explain anything to you. You and I shared, more or less, the same experiences. Help me and give me cyanide. It won't do any harm. Like in the old days. One cannot know how long one will be able to carry on." Henjo looked down at me and got up and went to his desk. He opened some drawer, pulled out a little box and gave me two pills. "I give you two," he explained, "although one is quite sufficient. Hide each one of them separately, in a different spot, so that you will be able to remember and find at least one when you need it."

I thanked him and went back home. I put one pill in the drawer near my bed, and the other in the desk. Just in case.

Then in that vacation at Jelechowice before the war, there was another family, that of deputy mayor Zwerling. With Lila and Wili. Wili was given such an idiotic name after his grandfather, William Zukerkandel,[19] who was a well-known publisher throughout Galicia. I don't know if they are still alive because I haven't seen them for a long time.

■ More and more I grow convinced this diary business is the pinnacle of stupidity. Can it be just masochism. I cannot explain it otherwise. Years have passed, many years, the end of the road is drawing near, and I revisit those old wounds, tearing at them. It's incomprehensible.

Today on the way from work, I met Mr. Aspis. Once, years ago, he was our neighbor, but now he is so changed. He told me, crying, that in the akcja they took Barbara, a girl my age who was named after my grandmother. But his older daughter, Regina, is alive and working. He himself has blackened terribly and put on lots of weight. Mother says that he is bloated from hunger.

■ The art of writing is the know-how of implanting: the ability to assemble or to dismantle, and of course, passing on pictures, situations, human characteristics, happenings. . . .

Observing today, from the side, that meeting with Mr. Aspis. He had never been tall, but already then he had shrunk to the height of a boy. Before the war, he was a craftsman who struggled through hard times with a good deal of suffering, but he lived, fought, fed his family, and was a human being. How should one write about him? How can one build a monument of letters, of words? Whole families were eradicated. There is no living soul that can remember.

Words are the only monument. What are they worth, what is the strength? But maybe it's forbidden to demand too much?

All of them, like Mr. Aspis, like his daughter Barbara, died twice. The first time when they were murdered and years later when they were forgotten. And that happens to a people that gives thanks to its past and tradition.

They have instituted a project called "Everyone has a name." Had. Had but no more. Another name erased.

Sunday, September 28th — *Mother along with Wartenberg and Uncle Lipa have been looking for contacts in order to get Aryan papers. We even got photographed the day before yesterday.*

■ A short time after the war, it seems to me in 1946, I had to go to Lodz. In those days a trip on the train was not particularly recommended. The Polish partisans used to stop trains, pull the Jews out, lead them to a dark field and shoot them. Therefore, I preferred to go by bus, because at that time I had never heard about a bus being stopped, not to mention the fact that buses drove in daylight. At the station in Gdansk the "bus" was already waiting: a mere truck that had been slightly touched up and turned into a kind of coach. It did not have much space and the passengers were few: a young woman, a young guy, a couple that probably was not a couple at all because they were not sitting together, somebody else resembling a priest, and also a farmer with a huge fair moustache and a basket of chickens. Ahead of me sat a fat non-Jewish woman who looked like a fishmonger in the market. The bus was relatively rapid, stopped only once to refuel, and after some five hours we arrived in Lodz. The station happened to be near the Jewish Community Board and all the passengers, all of them, went straight to that building. Even the couple who was not sitting together marched there arm in arm. Maybe the driver was also Jewish, but I didn't notice where he was going. . . .

But that cost lots of money and we cannot afford it. So Mother talked with Hryc and Marisia about hiding us in Jelechowice. We will move over there if there is an akcja or even if the atmosphere becomes too hot. Hryc came with a wagon and took a few things with him. Especially the winter clothes and other objects that were not so necessary. We moved the contents of the dining room into the house of our Ukrainian neighbor, Karpowa.

■ Was it an unexplained optimism, or just stupidity, to believe that a day would arrive on which again furniture would be needed, and it would be possible to use the property that had been accumulated for years or even generations?

Monday, October 9th — *The day before yesterday, in the evening, just after Mother had left for the Wartenbergs, she came back with the news of a terrible panic in town. Müller has arrived from Tarnopol with the Gestapo. Mother couldn't make up her mind whether to go to Hryc or wait until tomorrow. I supported going despite the time — 8 o'clock — and the beginning of the curfew. We put on warm clothes, took a bag with bread and sugar and set off. A heavy rain poured and the winds were too powerful for the umbrella to open. We just arrived at the Officers' Residence when we heard shots. Mother stopped in fear and wanted to return. But I managed to talk her into going on. By our warehouse we suddenly saw someone with a flashlight and we hid among the scraps of iron. After waiting for awhile we resumed our walk through the Jewish Quarter, passed Ritter's windmill and from there through Blich and the fields, up to our knees in mud, to Jelechowice. The night, the darkness, the rain, the wind, the mud and the fear — I'll never be able to forget that night.*

■ True: I've not forgotten. But if I'm not wrong the diary never mentioned that the distance between Zloczow and Jelechowice is merely four kilometers —the distance between my house and the sea on Shabbat walks. It's not a great distance, but enough to make me hate — to this very day — darkness, and particularly darkness with rain. It always arouses in me a sense of total insecurity. Not to mention causing me to lose an important component of romanticism.

By the way, on my visit to Zloczow I discovered that the light in the streets is quite frugal.

Finally we arrived and knocked on the door. Hryc and Misia were still awake because they were writing a letter to Mrs. Skerzeszewska. Hryc immediately made a fire, warmed milk and we went to bed. In the morning he went to town and found out all was quiet. Despite Misia's pleading that we should move over to them we returned home in the morning. We came back to agitation, fear and panic. We learned that a rumor was circulating about us being held in the Fortress. In that way people explained to themselves our sudden disappearance.

■ Maybe that's the true value of the diary: the documentation of the changes we were going through. For example, take my mother, a pampered woman who always was busy meeting her girlfriends and exclusively in charge of the daily run of the household. Suddenly she has turned into a person responsible for survival and the future, feeder, keeper of the flame. And she did all that naturally, as if it were her life-long occupation.

Thursday, October 16th — *I'm tired all the time. My work at the warehouse is exhausting: loading the trucks, weighing the "goods," registering everything. And when I come back home I find non-stop "club activity." The house is always full of acquaintance and friends. They stay late, "dabble in politics," and argue. They must enjoy being with us. Yesterday it was said at the "club" that Wehrmacht headquarters announced that following fierce battles in Stalingrad the Germans managed to occupy a room with kitchen facilities.*

■ The Germans managed to reach Stalingrad after being in power for ten years. If the world let them exist for ten more years, the American tourists would have traveled to Europe instead of the Sahara desert because the European climate would be much more clement.

The obsessive tinkering with the diary keeps returning me backward. Possibly the past — which already happened and therefore is safe — is closer to my heart than the future. Maybe because I don't believe in the future, not at all. What exists is only the present. And the past? All of us are filled with crumbs of contacts with people, with shreds of events that occurred in the past.

Yesterday, on Yom Kippur, I was eating, as usual, nuts. Of course I didn't fast. I had finished my quota of fasts a long time ago. I sat on the porch, digging for pieces of fruit among the broken shards, and remembered that it had all begun in my childhood. We, the children, always used to play with nuts by the wall of the Jewish Orphanage in Zloczow. On holidays one of the halls of the orphanage would be converted into a synagogue.

A few years ago I was sitting on my porch in Tel Aviv and cracking nuts. I was surprised when cars began driving in Arlosoroff Road. More and more cars. An incomprehensible phenomenon on Yom Kippur. But about an hour later the air raid sirens explained it all. They took advantage of my preoccupation with nut cracking and tried to liquidate me. Again. They failed, but they don't lose hope.

If they succeed one of those days, somebody else will sit on a porch somewhere and will be destined to remember.

Tuesday, November 4th — *On the first day of the month, a holiday, Misia and Hryc came to us for lunch. They kept pleading with us to finally come over to them. Next morning, before I had time to get up, Mrs. Reichard knocked on the door screaming, "they're catching in town!" I rushed into my clothes and followed Mother running to Karpowa. She tried to soothe us by saying they were catching people for forced labor in Germany and she was aware of that for some days now. But out her window we saw Schupo policemen leading Jews away. So we stole to Mrs. Lewek and climbed the ladder to the hideout. The Wartenbergs and Kiewetz with Celek were already there. Out a crack in the boards we saw groups of Germans looking for Jews in the street and it seemed to me that I could identify Dr. Burski in one of the groups.*

■ Years later I saw a similar picture in a western: walking in the street with the eager faces of righteous people set on running the bad ones down to earth, smoking together, joking together. Also a similar scene in the Warsaw ghetto in Wladyslaw Szlengel's mocking poem "Juno sind rund."[20]

A few years later a Jewish tribunal in Lodz boycotted that above-mentioned doctor. It did not help him that he assisted the hungry in those times, always serving them with soup from his kitchen, and there were many hungry, many needy people.

The tribunal forced him to travel all over the world and the Jews, dispersed everywhere, refused to let him join any community.

Why did he walk with an ax in his hand looking for hiding Jews? What made him do it? What was the reason?

In the evening the neighbor Glowaski brought news: terrible things are happening in town. The members of the Judenrat were taken as well but not before they took part in the akcja. They collected women, children, and old people! That story crushed us. A day later Karpowa brought us food and a friend of Wartenberg's, the Polish sergeant-major Malewski, came to boost our morale. Only this morning we emerged from the hideout, looking as if we came out of a chimney. Our apartment looks like a battlefield. Everything's a mess, scattered around, destroyed. Among other missing items is my watch that managed to survive the school's via dolorosa but succumbed to the akcja. Seven kilograms of cube sugar (prepared for the village), all of the silver cutlery, all handkerchiefs (except six of Mother's and mine), 60 eggs that Mother bought a day before the akcja, butter, bread, and so on and so forth.

■ Dr. Hreczanyk gave the watch to me when I was four. He came to visit me when I was sick with the flu and was amazed at my ability to "read" a watch. The doctor went out and returned half an hour later with a small, cute, lady watch, nice for a child. He, too, disappeared. . . .

Years later Dr. Hreczanyk became the personal doctor of Uberstubahnfüehrer Franz Warzog, the commander of Camp Lackie. When Warzog was moved to another position, to command Camp Janowski in Lvov, he took Dr. Hrezcanyk, his wife and son, along with him. He promised to protect them and let no one kill them; if need be, he'd do it himself. Warzog kept his promise.

Once upon a time to come, when I am seated on a cloud, I'll look downward and feel sorry then that I was born too early and in too bad a place, and my life was as it was.

Therefore it's odd, practically incomprehensible, that in my translation I've been doing all I can to will my thoughts to future readers.

Thursday, November 6th — *Everybody is running about looking for contacts in order to get Aryan papers. Escape — that's the dominant thought. We're immersed in stress and despair. Mother says we've been left without any family. She exaggerates as usual, because it's not exactly correct. I told her that. True, in the last akcja they took Uncle Friedmann — he won't invite me to the Passover Seder any longer, if there'll ever be another Passover or Seder.*

■ After the liberation we found out that the news wasn't precise. The Germans didn't send Uncle Friedmann to Belzec. His neighbors buried him alive in his courtyard.

And they took Uncle Kogut who had a free entrance to movie theaters and so I was able to see lots of movies. But his daughter Clara got married in Warsaw before the war. Maybe she was saved there. Or the Horowitz family from Lvov — we don't know anything about their fate. And Father's cousin, the one who's the head or the commander of the Papal Guard, surely only prays. The other cousin, Attorney Jorisch, who nowadays is a shoemaker in Brussels, fares better there than in Vienna. Or the cousin from Canada, Rosenbaum, now called Morton, the railway millionaire who wanted to adopt me — he also lives. Even if all the Jews of Zloczow are liquidated, far and near, or in the whole of Poland, or even in the whole of occupied Europe under Hitler's rule — Jews will be left in America and in Palestine. So what if they liquidated our neighbors, Dr. Reichard and his family? Their son is a pioneer in a kibbutz.

■ What an irony: he was sent to Palestine as a punishment. He was uncontrollable, unbearable, and so, despite the pain involved, they bid him farewell and sent him to the arid, wild country.

His family remained in green, civilized Europe.

There, in the kibbutz, he'll stay on. Also Chaplin, also Einstein. They'll yet dance over Hitler's grave. Jews have always been liquidated. There's nothing new about that. It's something Mother doesn't comprehend. Who are we anyway? A comma in History. When I was reading With Fire and Sword[21] *I talked to Father about Chmielnicki[22] existing in history only because of the thousands of Jewish and Polish victims that he slaughtered. This is our revenge. Hitler, too, will enter History because of us. Despite that I wish I could watch the aftermath. Just curiosity. If at the age of 14 I went through and saw so many things — the aftermath can be interesting as well. One thing I've decided for sure: if by any chance I manage to escape liquidation, I'll never marry. It's easier to survive when you're alone. Not to mention the children who come into the world as the result of the wedding. And that's absolutely redundant. One has to silence them with cyanide and that's too complicated and too expensive.*

■ Even now, more than fifty years after those words were written, too often I think that the world doesn't deserve to exist any longer. But I have children, and they have children, and therefore I find it impossible to scribble some cynical comment regarding those fifty years old words. Though I envy those of the unnumbered skin, as thick as an elephant's. A skin of the Holocaust PR experts, the writers who make money out of that kind of writing. Or those who make their livelihood by reviewing the books of professional Holocausters.

But more and more I discover the effect of the diary, the effect of the boy who wrote it on my present thinking. Something like schizophrenia.

Tuesday, November 11th — *The establishment of a ghetto was declared in town. Since the last akcja there's a daily panic in Zloczow. Today, in the afternoon, we came to the village of Jelechowice. We'll stay here. We received Helena's room. It's big and pretty. Tomorrow Hryc and I will build a hideout under the floor, behind the sofa.*

■ Thus, in a grave-like pit, narrow and long, was the beginning of the peaceful rural life. I couldn't imagine that the stay would be so long, that this place would suck me in and sink me deeply in the Holocaust whirlpool; that the era would affect my whole life; and the pictures from there would be etched in my memory forever — also with the help of the diary.

Sunday, November 16th — *Today Wasyli arrived, Hryc's brother-in-law and the former head of the village of Gologory. He came because the village's grocery store was "clean shaved" and he is the main suspect (he's a well-known thief). He doesn't know about our existence, so we hide from him as we do from other people. In the afternoon Marisia Tarnawska came visiting and Mother put on the garb of a nun (belonging to Misia's mother) and went to town with her to pick up objects that for some reason were left behind in our apartment.*

■ Today I think it was either an act of courage or of utter stupidity on Mother's part — to go to Zloczow where she knew everyone and everyone knew her, even disguised as a nun. Probably pieces of furniture had some value in those days. Later on, the years of Hitlerite education made it clear how unimportant all of that was.

Monday, November 17th — *Hryc went to town and at the very moment he came back with our things the neighbor Zagorski happened to be sitting in the kitchen. Before Zagorski had time to ask anything, Misia said to Hryc, "Has my cousin Renia sent all my things?" Hryc said, "I think so," and put it all in the room where I was sitting silently. He winked at me and I winked back.*

■ Some years ago I went to Poland for a first visit since I had left in 1957. Naturally I paid a visit to Hryc, the only one among my saviors who was still alive. "You are my relatives," sobbed the lonely man, happy to meet me, "the Jews I had saved scattered all over the world, some went to America, some to Israel. I didn't believe I'd be lucky to yet see somebody from my family. . . ."

Tuesday, November 18th — *Sitting at lunch we heard Rex barking. Looking out the window we saw Mrs. Skrzeszewska! Of course I ran to the room thinking, "That's exactly what we needed!" Mother wasn't there and I was certain we would be thrown out. I listened by the door and heard Misia and Helena crying. I didn't understand why. Suddenly they began to whisper. Hryc came, called me and I went in. Helena opened her arms and said, "How are you? Now we share the same situation." I asked why and she explained that they wanted to arrest her husband. He shot at them, killed a German and of course ran away. Now he was hiding with some gardener in Lvov. Before evening fell, when Helena and Misia and Grandma were sitting in their room and Hryc with Wasyli in the kitchen, I heard knockings on the porch. Hryc went to open it and I heard him explaining to Wasyli that it was a friend of Misia's. I guessed Mother came back. Immediately after Wasyli went to sleep at Stanislawski's I entered Misia's room and saw Mother talking to them about the problems of Helena's husband. When we returned to our room Mother said we did well to escape from Zloczow and that there was no room for worry because here everything was all right.*

■ All right? Today I'm not sure at all. What does it mean, "we did well to escape from Zloczow?" Did anything new happen? Why did she keep some of the information from me? If she would have done that — certainly I would have entered it in the diary. She treated me as a child who should better be kept ignorant of certain things. I wasn't a child regarding forced labor, but still a child regarding other aspects? Did they not notice I had grown up? Maybe not yet. I still was short, with no beard, but definitely not a child any more.

That duality existed until liberation. As if the very fact of becoming free stamped me with the mark of maturity. Perhaps my growing tall helped. It's not easy to treat a long, thin "macaroni" like a child.

Friday, November 21st — The day before yesterday Mother gave Helena a suit of Father's for her husband and she went away. Life has returned to routine. We walk about the house without any inhibition, trusting Rex to faithfully do his duty. He barks differently at anyone so we can know in advance whether he's a friend or a foe. In any case, whenever we hear him, Mother and I enter our room, shut the door and Misia, if the visitor is a stranger, sings "Chiming of Bells in the Dusk." Then we sit quietly, almost without breathing, waiting for the visit to end. Nobody must know about our existence here.

■ I didn't have the stamina to go on translating. So, in the early hours of the afternoon, I went to the beach. Lots of people were there, tanning their

Fragment of music for "Chiming of Bells in the Dusk"

skins, playing ping-pong, gallivanting in the water. I rented an easy chair, settled down comfortably, and looked around. I was relaxed, feeling well. Close to me, by the water, sat a not so young woman, her legs spread, letting the waves penetrate the harbor. I intentionally ignored her constant looks at me. Two boys came up to me.

"Grandpa," said one of them, "give us a cigarette."

"I can't," I said, "because I'm not your grandfather. And certainly I wouldn't give cigarettes to my grandchildren."

They stood there for a moment, looked at me, and moved off.

I was glad to remember that, because a minute ago it seems that my mind had gone blank, and only now came back.

I am not focused. My thoughts are disorderly. An association pursues an association. Later it's difficult, even impossible, to peel off the layers and reach the basic, original idea. Even now I thought . . . wait a minute, what was it? I can't remember.

Maybe it's old age. Or some mental disturbance. Certainly it's not pleasant.

Only at night can one get out and Hryc, to my great delight, takes advantage of that. He takes me to the forest to steal trees. We take a big saw, two axes and set on our way to find a "victim." Oak is the best because it's harder than pine. Sawing on both sides we manage to crash it down, then cut off the branches, slice the trunk into several logs and drag them home. Next morning, if possible, we saw and cut the logs into firewood for the kitchen or the ovens in the rooms. It's wonderful work. Sometimes peasants arrive from distant villages. Then we go out to them and barter. That way we bartered a winter blanket with a pillowcase, two pillows, and a variety of clothes, for food. What really matters is getting food. Our hosts don't take money from us for our stay (except gifts!), but we take care of feeding everybody.

■ Barter is the ancient foundation of all commerce. It has come back in one of the blackest periods in the history of the human race. Existence was based on it and yet it did have some funny moments. One of our acquaintances exchanged his piano for the meat of half a pig (of course he sold most of it). The farmer told him that that piece of furniture would be very convenient at the chicken-coop because the chickens would sit on the wires and the eggs would drop on the plate.

Monday, December 8th — I have reading material. It's very important because what else can one do here? It's rather difficult to be in jail. When I look in the direction of Zloczow I remember the words of Mickiewicz,[23] "My country . . . how much you should be prized only he can learn / who has lost you."

■ My country? What country?

Yes, I was born in Poland, but is she my country? I felt like a guest there. Centuries but still a guest. Does somebody born on a boat wear a sailor uniform all his life? Isn't this writing in Hebrew a proof of something? Kafka wrote that language has the sound of the motherland breathing.

But I can't explain the meaning of "writing." I have to thank the method and customs that dominate my writing. Every few lines, every few thoughts contained in the diary — I stop, slide down in the chair to a half reclining position, and discover a supply of pictures on the ceiling. The magic power of the diary, like a time machine, takes me backward. Of course, I could limit myself to translation, no comments, and thus keep the continuity of the narrative (it's no innovation: cutting it has been known for more than a century) — but something inexplicable has dictated to me that writing form. What does it prove?

Obviously, the lack of home is a terrible thing, because even if the war draws to an end I doubt we'll have anywhere to return to. But let it end. In the meanwhile I enjoy Misia's huge chest of books and magazines. Most of it is professional literature like the weekly The Teacher's Voice *or Catholic weeklies like* The Virgin's Knight. *There are regular books or stories cut out of newspapers. In* The Teacher's Voice *I found a four years old interesting research conducted among kids my age. Only the Jewish students responded to the question "what would you like to be?" using one and only one word: famous. If it's so it means that I'm an ordinary Jewish boy.*

■ A Jew remains a Jew — always, whether he wants it or not, for better or worse. It reminds me of Einstein who said: "If I succeed the Germans will say I'm a German and the French will say that I'm a citizen of the world. If I fail the Germans will announce that I'm Jewish and the French that I'm a German."

Thursday, December 25th — *Today is Christmas. Last night we had a holiday dinner. Mother made lots of good things: borsht with mushroom dumplings, wonderful pirogi, French cookies, a honey*

cake, kutia [Ukrainian sweet], vodka. After the meal we sang
Christmas carols. One song used new words to the melody of
"Today in Bethlehem." (Today in London, today in London there is
a great news: one thousand bombers, one thousand bombers flew
to Berlin; Berlin is burning, Hamburg is falling, the Wehrmacht is
fleeing, Hitler is screaming, great news!)

■ When I now read the description of that so Polish scene, I think that our joint expedition in history started on the wrong foot and remained so to this very day. The Poles were first mentioned in writing by a Jewish merchant,[24] the name of their first king was etched in Hebrew letters on the coins, and independent Poland of the post-First-World-War years was declared in the late lamented Chelm, a pearl in the annals of Jewish folk humor. . . .

Not to mention our inconsiderate behavior — we evacuated Poland and left its people without the traditional scapegoat. The first to leave, millions of Jews, vanished without a trace. The second wave, at the end of the Forties, left because they didn't want to live in a graveyard. The third wave, composed of those who were refused a permit to leave with the previous wave, left with me at the end of the Fifties. And the fourth and final wave took along all those who believed that Poland changed but were bitterly disappointed. So today Poland is seeped with anti-Semitism but empty of Jews.

The Jewish Polish writer Bruno Jasienski[25] wrote that things happen only thanks to human indifference. Not to know, not to do anything, is a kind of involvement. And that was characteristic of Polish behavior during the Holocaust.

1943

January 20th — *After New Year's day Grandma [Misia's mother] fell sick and a couple of days ago the decline began. A day before her death she told me, "You must be healthy (I pulled a muscle in my neck). I am already suffering for both of you. And don't forget to convert to Christianity." She loved Mother and me very much but couldn't forgive us for not being Christian.*

■ Despite her pleadings I haven't converted. I don't know why. True, I knelt and prayed every evening, but was it really faith? I'm afraid it was mainly the wish to conform.

I doubt Christianity is the solution. Even if it did open a door to an escape from Judaism, from persecutions, from humiliation.

An Egyptian proverb says that a log won't change into a crocodile even after one hundred years of immersion in the Nile. I haven't seen or heard of anybody successfully escaping from Judaism. Even when one tried to forget, sooner or later he remembered his origins or was reminded.

Even if he was a cardinal. . . .

Grandma was very religious and prayed for entire days. She died three days ago, at dawn. We immediately arranged the room, put up a special table on which we dressed her in nun's attire. Grandma belonged to the Third Order of the Franciscans. All the time neighbors came to pray and naturally we were shut in the room. In the morning Misia's brother arrived with his son and Rena with her husband. We entered the hideout under the floor, because the priest and the family were sitting in our room. There was a little problem with Rex who sensed my presence and pushed at the sofa standing over us. Hryc threw him out of the room. After the funeral, Helena returned first and we came out, rearranged everything and again were able to begin a normal life.

■ When I cannot fall asleep I go out to the porch. My street is dark and quiet, only the old trees are darker than dark. Cars go past and the stars peep from among the roofs. They seem closer than they were in my childhood. I light a cigarette and think what would have happened if I were born in another time, another place, another family? Would my life have been better? Is it certain I would have been born to a rich duke? And been blond?

What is done cannot be reversed and one mustn't complain. I feel deep in my heart that here I have a city and in the city a street and in the street a house and in the house an apartment and in the apartment this room with the desk and in the desk a chaotic drawer with redundant things: a key (for what?), a ticket (to where?) and so on and so forth — like in Tuwim's[26] poem — leftovers of the past, memories, life. If I'm allowed to quote Brenner[27] — I don't have another place. It has become consciously clearer, emotionally better felt, while translating the diary.

February 2nd — Helena travels all the time on the Zloczow-Kopyczynce-Lvov line and trades in whatever she can lay her hands on. She also brings news from the world. The Germans were screwed in Stalingrad, liquidated. They deserve it. Perhaps that's the beginning of the end, perhaps?

■ Almost every evening, when Helena stayed at home, we had rural entertainment. "Putting Up a Kabala."[28] You spread a pack of cards over the table, and the whole future, the length and width of destiny, are there in front of you. One has only to read correctly and use a special language, for example, when the fellow of dreams will return from a trip it's possible that an official personality will pay a visit, following which all participants will be invited to the fortress. Translated into a human language it sounds quite simple: when the husband returns, a policeman will arrive and arrest everybody and put them in jail.

Very optimistic, just in the spirit of the time.

But to this very day I don't know why it's called "kabala," with the Polish emphasis on the last but one syllable.

Is this, too, a Jewish conspiracy?

Sunday, February 15th — *It was definitely embarrassing. A few minutes ago, when Hryc went to church in town, Misia called out to me from their room. I went in and saw her sitting there in a nightgown of Milanese cloth, pink and transparent. Her right leg was slightly raised and didn't hide the deep shadow down the slope of her belly. She suggested I sit by her saying, "I'd like to give you a little test." I flushed and said that maybe later, because now I was writing something important, please forgive me, and escaped to our room. Mother raised her eyes from her sewing and gave me a strange look.*

■ It seems to me that then, and possibly today, I was writing out of distress. Now, like then, writing is a kind of escape from reality. In my case, translating the diary is an escape to a time without worries. Or rather: time that revolved around one worry only — survival. All the rest became minute or even faded away. It's also a proof that the Russian saying is right: you'll go on living but won't feel like fucking.

Immediately I sat down to write, to scribble; I'm upset by the thought I might have made a mistake. What, after all, could have happened if I stayed? Misia is a teacher, if I wouldn't know anything, she'd have taught me. My only consolation is that subconsciously I was unable to approach her — she's so old and ugly! And a kiss! Brrr . . . if it were Zula — well, I haven't seen her for three months. I wonder if she's in the ghetto.

■ Zula. Tall, with a halo of chestnut curls; blue eyes shaded by long eyelashes; the first I made love to — we kissed; childishly naïve we feared it was the beginning of pregnancy; two years later Zula was killed, 14 years old.

A requiem for Zula. Her father was murdered in the very first pogrom; she lived with her little sister and her mother who tried to feed all three of them; it was difficult because she wasn't local and also sickly and pampered, used to a rich life in Katowice. The Germans caught up with them in Zloczow. Zula and her family were liquidated with the rest of the ghetto.

A requiem for Zula. She was ordered into forced labor at the age of 13; a young neighbor, whose wife and children were taken to Belzec in one of the akcjas, saved her; he remained on his own in his spacious apartment, adopted Zula and instructed her, took care to provide the right customers, lonely as he, craving a little feminine warmth. Zula's reputation preceded her and a long line of clients registered with the neighbor. That way Zula was able to honorably (yes, yes!) provide for her family.

A requiem for Zula. Who lived her life out at an accelerated pace. A requiem . . .

Or maybe Zula, too, managed to escape. Or Clara, her friend. We first kissed at her place, behind the door of her father's tin works. How excited we were! How old were we? 12?

■ About a month ago I visited a Zloczowan love temple at Kempa. A wooded mound with benches and no lights. In the summer evenings it was absolutely dark. One could only hear whispers. I, too, in my memories kept faith with tradition and kissed a girl there. How old were we? That was our first kiss, but it seems that for Clara it was the last one as well.

In the diary the story is somewhat different. Does memory always play tricks with us, beautifying the past?

Or Krystyna Pawlak, the Sergeant-Major's daughter, whom I loved from first grade until the war. Strange how I forgot all about her and remembered her only now. The Soviets must have sent her to Siberia. There are such vast spaces but God or Fate might cause her to run into Ruta Werker. I'll serve them as a common subject. I smiled, remembering how Father, when he saw Ruta for the first time on the street, before I even had time to say "she's my girl-friend," already knew she had thick ankles. As a matter of fact, it's no wonder. Even before I went to elementary school my grandfather taught me that women should be observed from bottom to head: first the legs, then the hands, finally the eyes. If those are nice, everything is O.K. All other components are identical in all women. I hope he knew what he was saying. Maybe I'll be able to find out myself one day.

■ A Polish writer once told me that if one has talent but not a sense of humor, it's better to be cured of talent as one is cured of a runny nose. There are doubts regarding my talent, but I hope that at least I've retained a sense of humor. It's a fact that I don't treat myself or my writing too seriously.

February 25th — Yesterday we stopped being a branch of the Spirits Monopoly. I've a terrible headache from tasting the product: we produced more than eight liters of samogon [homemade vodka]. The first drops, the first bottle, were very powerful, real spirits. While dripping for a duration the percentage of alcohol went down and finally the water was very weak. What was fascinating was the work itself. First we mixed potatoes with grain and added yeast.

That fermenting dough stood and stank for a long time. Then Hryc borrowed a vat with pipes from the neighbors. We put the vat on the plate in the kitchen and after boiling and then cooling off for some time, drops began falling into the bottle. Finally, a yellow, somewhat dry dough smelling of alcohol remained. It was a pity to have to throw it away, so Hryc scattered a bit in the yard for the chickens and the rest he put in the trough for the cow Krasula. vThe chickens pecked — and immediately lay down on the earth, absolutely foggy minded. But Krasula started going berserk, running around and climbing trees. It was terribly funny but also a bit dangerous. Hryc managed to overcome her with much difficulty and tied her up in the stable.

I needed no binding having fallen asleep in a corner of the room. Like the chickens.

■ The café on Main Street. A place — so they told me once — where people do nothing, only drink alcohol or coffee and chat. I remember my uncle liked to visit there. I also remember how in 1941 the town had experienced a sensation: a line of German cars parked by the cafe. Uniformed Germans were strolling there and even then I noticed they didn't know how to talk, shouting all the time. It was a delegation arriving to pick up the German communists who had fled from Hitler to Soviet Russia and now Stalin helped return them to their motherland.

February 26th *— Today is a nice day and Helena took me to the garden to clean the wood patch. Hryc and Misia were very angry with me for strolling outside in the middle of a clear day. In truth it can be danger- ous, but I enjoyed spending time in the fresh air and work- ing. The world seems different that way than when one looks at it from behind the window, from behind the curtain. . . .*

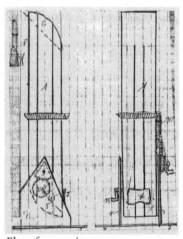

Plans for a periscope

Once, when the Soviets were here, I built a periscope. It was a simple job: four pieces of wood with two mirrors, one at each end. Leszek Dywer gave the mirrors to me. When I asked him if he had anything of the sort he answered in the negative, but that he would have it in a jiffy. He took me to their living room, picked up a chair and threw it at a huge mirror covering half the wall. It broke and he gave me two pieces of true Belgian glass. My periscope functioned well, but the one I invented today, in the air, is far more advanced.

■ Strange are the ways of evolvement. Since I was a child it was clear that my future was bound with technology, that I would become an engineer or something like that. I loved building things, inventing, drawing. And despite that past I changed direction completely and moved from technology over to the humanities. In that sphere, too, I invented new things (in my eyes) and I'd like to believe that I also built something new.

March 3rd — Yesterday Linka came to us to check the situation. She lives with her family outside the ghetto but they are terrified of the liquidation despite having managed to get Aryan papers. Helena has been trying to talk them into moving in with us. Linka gave Hryc leather for boots but both Misia and he are not enthusiastic about the idea. Misia is Hryc's lover, which disturbs Helena, because once he was her lover. On the other hand Misia was Karol's lover and he is Helena's husband.

■ I found that erotic convolution strange, to use an understatement. Everybody with everybody — they aren't even embarrassed in their daily contacts. Today it seems to me that Helena needed sex as an expression of life. Because of various arrangements I happened to share a room with her for the night and every time she would take off her clothes without paying any attention to me. I was amazed at her young girl body and I found it disturbing that she treated me as if I was her son. Was it a kind of Oedipus complex? Hers or mine?

Misia is smooth and nice on the outside but really she's a bad woman who "works" on Hryc all the time. He's not a bad guy but weak, ignorant and somewhat unstable. Helena is undoubtedly a good woman but tense. It's bad when they're together. One could have managed each one of them alone. Linka wasn't happy about the atmosphere here but I think she has no alternative. I doubt it'll improve our lot when they arrive, five people, including an old mother and two little girls — but there's no other choice: we have to do our best to help them. The trouble is that Misia doesn't allow Hryc to take their things when he goes to town.

■ Suddenly, while writing, without any warning, I was beset with pains in the chest, on the left side. Is it the heart or the lungs? Should I stop smoking? It'll be hard for me, I won't be able to write even one word without a cigarette, but on the other hand, if I don't stop and then have a heart attack or contract cancer, I'll not finish this job. Who'll finish it? Such a pity to lose it all. If I could co-ordinate the end of writing with the ultimate end . . . . Memento Mori? Well, is it really important?

I begin to suspect that the diary isn't important either.

March 31st — Beyond the road, between the summer resort of the high school and the military shooting range a few trucks arrived, loaded with French P.O.W.s who are digging pits. Zagorski went to have a look and said that probably they're going to build fortifications there. That's exactly what we need. With the Soviet precision of bombing and our luck we'll be the first to go. It's not funny at all to be killed by one's liberators. I'm not an expert on strategy but why do they dig in the valley and not in the hills around? If the pits are as big as Zagorski claims they will serve as bunkers for the headquarters. If we live, we'll see.

■ Another surprise in the diary: in my memory this period is etched as one big bore. All the time the same walls, the same faces, the same house arrest. But the truth is that all the time something was happening, and always something ominous. All the time there was news, the best of which was quickly refuted as mere gossip. It seems it's hard not to get damaged under such a daily steam roller.

April 2nd — About 10 o'clock Helena and Hryc returned from Kopyczynce.[29] The moment the door opened I knew something had happened. Helena turned to Hryc and said, "Didn't I tell you that they don't know?" Mother asked what happened and Helena replied, "Nothing, only the liquidating akcja of the Jews in the ghetto." You may well imagine how we received the news. Mother grew pale and entered our room and I followed her. Besides the other Jews our only living relative, Linka, was there. We were broken hearted. I told Mother that if anything happened to Linka and the girls it would be exclusively Misia's fault.

■ It's difficult to accept that the writer of the diary was a boy, a teenager who was supposed to go on living a complete life, maybe even happy.

More and more I identify with myself in that time. More and more I think like that boy in the diary. I'm afraid that at the end of the translation we'll become one. And even worse, we'll have the same mind. Maybe it's a good idea to slow the pace of the work, because it seems its end will be mine as well.

April 3rd — *After a sleepless night, but a night full of crying, Helena rushed to town in the morning to find out what happened to the aunt. Mother was so nervous she was unable to do anything, not even eat. At noon Helena came back with the news that Linka and her family were hiding, but their neighbor Anna Kopystynska refused to tell where. Mother slightly relaxed but kept repeating that they would surely be found in time if not already. Helena told terrible stories. The Jews were loaded on trucks and taken to a clearing in a pine forest near us, beyond the road. Between the summer resort of the high school and the shooting range, the place where a few days ago the French P.O.W.s were digging "fortifications." So those were the German fortifications. And we thought the shots sounded from the range. . . .*

■ Today I'm not impressed by bad news, not at all. The fear in me has been eroded. It's a pity because fear has some good aspects as well. Napoleon said that fear unites human beings. I saw how frightened people did something, acted to improve their situation. It was like that over there. It's like that here, too. When a ruler in the neighborhood waves his sword, people defend themselves out of fear, and possibly that's the reason why they win. And I'm in a vacuum: all my feelings, including fear, have vanished.

That's why I'm happy to read a newspaper every day. Here's the proof that nothing changes and I don't have to cope with something unexpected or unfamiliar.

Anda told Helena that the ghetto was surrounded at dawn. First they went to those who had a permit to live outside the wall. Only then the akcja began inside the ghetto. The first to be taken were the members of the Judenrat whose offices were at the Rosenzweig house across from the ghetto. Zagorski, who — as a former postman — knew people in Zloczow said he saw Dr. Glanz, Roza Henis, the dentist Braun and the mill owner Brandt led to liquidation. That's terrible! Horrendous! All Jews, all friends being killed and that so close to us and we . . . nothing . . . just live.

■ It's really close: beyond the road. I was there now. In the forest, some four kilometers from the town, where the ghetto is buried. Of course there's no tombstone, no sign, nothing to signify that thousands were buried here. But standing there I realized to what extent nature has proven the excellent quality of us as fertilizer. A particularly lush vegetation points to the mass graves.

And the military shooting range stands guard over their rest.

April 4th — Helena again visited the town and finally discovered that our people were hiding in the cellar at Anda's very place. They decided that Helena would bring them over to us.

■ How simple it sounds nowadays, "bring them over." Really, what was the problem? We said it was only four kilometers away. But is it possible to imagine today that in order to prevent the Jews from escaping the town was surrounded by a ring of soldiers, that there was a nightly curfew, that papers were checked at every corner.

Today I don't know if it was courage on Helena's part or just frivolity. Or both.

April 6th — Yesterday afternoon Helena went to town for the evening mass and was supposed to begin the project. Around 9 p.m. we heard knocking on the door. Naturally, we hid in the room and Misia went to open it. We heard Helena telling her to take the lamp from the kitchen. Then it became quiet. A few moments later Helena came in and took off her coat. Mother asked, "did you bring anyone of mine?" "Yes," she answered. "Who?" "Everybody." Upon hearing that Mother started trembling with excitement. We ran to Misia's room to embrace them. We were happy they were saved. We put them to bed and I, having no space for myself, was sitting up all night. All of them have arrived! In the morning they showed us the Aryan papers that had been bought in Warsaw under the name of Bolski. Lipa is called Stefan, Linka is Irena, Eda is Danuta and Selma is Krystyna. The pure Aryans! We concealed the papers in our secret place in the room.

■ There's no doubt I've become more Jewish after the Holocaust. Perhaps because I understood that I was facing two possibilities: to entirely assimilate or to make aliyah. I don't believe a survivor is capable of assimilating and escaping from his so Jewish memories. Innocently I thought that in disembarking from the ship in the Port of Haifa I could finally become a regular human being. But the world wouldn't let me. We cannot be "a nation like all other nations." All the time they demand that we be different. Therefore they treat us differently.

We are the Chosen People. . . .

April 8th — Life has become tense and restless. The girls have introduced an atmosphere of disorderliness and noise. Earlier I felt superbly in the village but now I've become nervous and unhappy. But there's no alternative, one has to help people, even at the expense of quiet and comfort. Linka is a good woman but as tense as the rest of us. Eda and Selma are wonderful girls but they don't want to eat. A real riot.

■ I was reminded of Sartre's play *No Exit* that I had seen years ago. I don't understand how it wasn't me who had written the play, or how Sartre could do it without being in Jelechowice. Is everyone who was there assured of inheriting Paradise when his time comes?

A propos, Lipa made it clear at the very beginning that an intelligent person was only one who read *Faust* in the original. What can I do, I read Goethe in the Polish translation, and even then I hardly understood it.

May 6th — During the last weeks life has started entering a peaceful mode. We moved over to a small room that formerly was Misia's. It's close to the hideout. With Hryc we built a hideout that we enter through the bottom of the closet in the porch, a bit of crawling and sitting in a kind of corridor or rather a trench from the last War. On top of us grow flowers and we can smell them from below. A preparation for things to come.

■ I take off my hat to myself. I thought I was becoming naïve but no, I became plain stupid. I realize it was I who invented the phrase "to smell the flowers from underneath." Well, also I. When I heard that phrase years later I laughed. I wonder if then, in 1943, it would have been a funny expression.

Today Helena returned from town with the news that Weinstock's wife was looking for a place in the village and she committed herself to finding her a hideout. The first person she applied to, Stanislawska, who lives not far from us, agreed to take Mrs. Weinstock in.

■ I stopped on Main Street where Weinstock's big confectionery store used to be. I remembered the place because it was the same house as the Pallas movie theater. Immediately on entering I realized the store changed. On one shelf stood a pair of rubber boots, another had a second-hand teddy bear, but in reasonably good condition, and yet another carried a few "Kilim" rugs[30] typical of that area. I bought a small one, a memento from the town of my birth. Walking out I found it was impossible to remember the kind of store that formerly joined Weinstock's — now they were selling dairy products, that's to say they were supposed to sell them. Because at the big store the upper shelves carried a few bottles of something that defied identification. The rest of the store, whose walls were covered with white porcelain, was simply empty. Just nothing with the exception of the saleswoman, and a sheet of paper with a list of prices in the store window.

May 7th — In the evening we heard a knocking on the door and someone entered quietly. That was odd because usually when somebody arrives Misia makes lots of noise to warn us and also to cover our potential sounds. I guessed it was Edzia Weinstock and indeed it was. Helena went out to take her over to Stanislawska.

■ Is my misanthropy an inbred characteristic or an outcome of that period of life registered in the diary? It seems to me that we load all the deficiencies and shortcomings on those times even if their seeds had certainly existed earlier. Possibly they had better developed in that "greenhouse."

May 9th — Yesterday Edzia came to visit us. She told terrible stories about the liquidation akcja. She herself learned about the akcja when the Germans and their accomplices came to the Judenrat building where they were living. Antoniak entered and ordered them to dress and wait for him. They could have taken advantage of that and hid themselves but didn't have the necessary wits. The gendarme came back, took Weinstock and other people and went away. The women hid in some hole on the second floor and at night moved over to the Jewish Hospital where they had a hideout. Edzia's brother, a Jewish policeman, brought her over from there to the Witlizky camp and from there she arrived at Stanislawska's.

■ All of the akcja stories indicate that once somebody was "taken" by the Germans that was the end of the story. Not at all! Why don't they tell about the long moments on the way to the assembly place?

About the waiting there, the way to the train depot, the journey in crammed cattle cars, the very last moments in the death camp. . . . The whole Via Dolorosa somehow disappears as in the report, which finds the term "taken" sufficient.

But maybe it's correct? Whoever was taken stopped existing at that moment.

Edzia also said that even Ludwig, the commander of the Gestapo in Zloczow, didn't know about the akcja. Edzia's husband was his "macher." The liquidation was conducted by the Gestapo and Schupo from Lvov. They took all our acquaintances and it's diffi-cult to find any survivors. After they took the Dywers their son Leszek, who was a friend of mine, helped the Germans to trace the hiding Jews! What scum! To inform on brothers! Those people should be tied to horses and torn to pieces or impaled on a stake! But in our world they live while the decent people are killed.

■ Quite understandably the Germans liquidated Leszek despite his services. I remember that in the Soviet period, while on vaca-tion from school, we decided, along with another friend, to earn some rubles by doing gardening jobs. On one of our noon breaks, while we were sitting on the grass and eating, Leszek turned to me and asked me to show him hair on the prick. I got up on my feet, went to Leszek and patted his head. Leszek became agitated but was afraid to react.

May 13th — Edzia came only "for one day to wash." Then came the second day, and the third, and she stayed forever. Since her arrival, intrigues and quarrels have begun. I can't stand her — from the very moment I set eyes on her. Mother found that each word uttered among us is passed on by Edzia to the landlords. She tells Misia what Helena says about her and to Helena what Misia says about her, to Mother she slanders Linka and so on and so forth. One comes to know people only when one lives with them. What's the saying? When eating a barrel of salt together. . . .

■ How childish it is! And how astonishing! But it was a good lesson in human relations. And I have to be grateful for learning what to expect from people. Today I'd certainly be prepared for such a behavior.

People with masks, with the cute masks glued to their faces. They look you straight in the eyes but their eyes are dead. They say they're honest but they lie. They fake. When I was young and at times drank too much I would walk along a straight line, the seam joining the floor boards, in order to prove that I wasn't drunk. I have never seen a sober man doing that. And that's how it goes with truth: who sticks to   it needs not emphasize it all the time. And the masked ball goes on.

The girls are very bored. I decided to do something to entertain them. I drew a kind of colored screw that when its spring is pulled it seemingly soars endlessly from a small box which lies under another small box. Regrettably the drawing isn't so good or the toy should be really built in order to entertain. In any case the girls didn't seem to understand what was going on and everything looked too abstract. What a pity.

Plans for a toy

■ Once I was walking with a friend in the environs of Gdansk, we visited the Crusaders' citadel. We were elated by the pastoral landscape and suddenly arrived at the ruins of the Stutthof camp,[31] where they manufactured soap. Only by mere chance I didn't serve as raw material.

If I were turned into soap I could have fallen into dirty hands, or with a bit of luck made a child happy by being colorful bubbles. I would have become agile, crumbled in the wind, completely disappeared, including my genes.

May 30th — I think it was a mistake: I painted a doll house for Eda and Selma, but they don't have dolls, and therefore a doll

*house is of no use to them. And it is just a failure playing "pretend."
And that's a doll house with all the accessories, even a water tower
and a power station.*

■ But — to the best of my memory — a cage with a canary was
missing. In the war my canary, Kubus, was transferred to the
kitchen and its best singing happened during the bombings. I took
care of it, fed it, cleaned the cage — and I don't know what
happened to it and where she disappeared. Did Mother give it to
anybody or was it stolen? I can't remember, like many other things.
Only the diary's testimonial helps. Besides that. . . .

June 6th — *Hryc takes something to exchange or at worst ten
gold dollars and buys 100 kilogram sacks each of black flour grits.
Then, in the afternoon, we make bread: in a big barrel we knead
the dough, light an oven to bake the bread and I turn into a baker.
I've got a long-long shovel and when the oven is opened the heat
emanates from it, I become an Indian and carefully push the
loaves inside. After an hour, when they are fresh, their taste is
wonderful.*

*Funny though that nobody is interested to know why for a
household of three Hryc buys everything in wholesale. Doesn't it
seem strange?*

■ Yesterday I was walking along Ibn Gabirol Street and ran into
Alexander. We went in to drink coffee and I told him about translating the diary. He said that he had gone through the war with a
false identity. It sounds like a joke with his Yiddish accented Polish,
with his looks. "I presented myself as a Lithuanian, I had no papers,
I had no money, but I was young and strong."

"And did it work?"

"You see, I escaped westward, to the Poznan region where Jews
were hardly known. I worked in the village, at the farm of somebody with four cows. A rich old man, maybe Polish, maybe
German. He didn't pay me anything. Thought he found a fool.

But does it matter? What matters is that he fed me, gave me some rags to wear, and I lived there like a king."

When the Soviets liberated the area Alexander told the Polish peasant that he was going back to Lithuania. But he really traveled to Lodz and from there managed to escape to Italy and then to Palestine. Only then he wrote a letter in which he briefly explained the truth. "My wife helped me write because my Polish is far from good. We had a good laugh imagining his face upon reading the letter."

I've known Alexander for many years and only now he told me his story. As long as our generation exists weird stories will surface about the survivors. But to the relief of future generations it's about to end. Soon.

June 7th — Our main occupation during most of the time is playing solitaire or card games. It's a quiet occupation, but how much can one do? In the mean- while it gave me an idea for a table clock. The back- drop of the board should — naturally! — be dark green. The frame, a chess board (chrome nickel and black lacquer), the hands like cards, also the hours

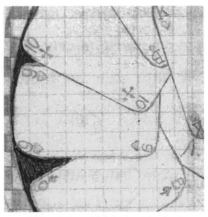

Drawing of the table clock with playing cards for numbers

(in order) and something to mark the precise hour. A pretty clock. I drew it.

■ I've a new explanation for that outburst of inventions: being cut off, and lacking activity, boredom. The world goes up in flames, masses of people are being killed — and we are closed in, isolated, living an allegedly "normal" life. Was it a kind of unconscious escape?

Or loss of sensitivity?

July 23rd — *Today they finally liquidated the Witlizky camp.*
Maybe they at last finished building the Atlantic Wall or just ran
out of ruined houses or found that they could manage without
Jews. After the ghetto was liquidated the remaining Jews deluded
themselves: they received a reprieve for several months, worked like
mules and in the end the Germans liquidated them as well.
Zloczow is left without Jews. I wonder how many are hiding like
us. In any case, living in Zloczow after the war will be like living in
a cemetery. At midnight the ghosts will howl. It's no consolation
that already five times Hitler was "assassinated" and three times a
revolution broke out and the regime in Germany has changed. The
end. The last Jews, the last Mohicans, are liquidated. All in all
about 6,000 Jews possibly remained in Zloczow before the final
phase and now all Jews (except a few, very few) are killed. And we
live, talk, laugh, eat — though after all these calamities, it would
have been more befitting to put ashes on our heads, or even hang
ourselves. But the impulse of survival is stronger. Now Edzia wants
to bring her brother over here. All the time she drives Misia nuts by
pleading, "let's build a hideout for my brother, let's build a
hideout." Skerzeszewski, who returned home a week ago, pounced
on the idea. Truly, he's a paranoid and drives us all nuts. All the
time, day and night, there are alerts. Constant tension. He escaped
with his friend Jakubowski who has been planning our new hide-
out. "Only for a couple of days, until it becomes more tranquil. . . ."

■ Years ago, on the way from Paris to London, we got off at the
train station in Calais. By the rail tracks I found remains of the
Atlantic Wall, bunkers which have not yet shed their camouflage
colors. I didn't feel any excitement despite the possibility that I per-
sonally knew some of the bricks used for building the bunkers. Not
to mention my proximity to the Zloczow brick factory where we
used to slide down the snowy slopes every winter.

I read a lot about the Atlantic Wall in the papers of our neighbors from the army of the Third Reich. In reality it didn't help them
much. Maybe it was only propaganda. And for that goal it was
worthwhile to transport bricks across Europe? Didn't they have

closer ruins? I begin to doubt the famous German organizational genius.

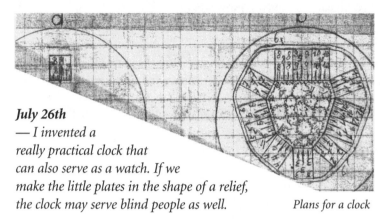

July 26th
— *I invented a
really practical clock that
can also serve as a watch. If we
make the little plates in the shape of a relief,
the clock may serve blind people as well.*

Plans for a clock

■ In our dining room at home stood a big, beautiful "Gdansk" clock (one can understand my sudden association) that ticked away, a clock that had lots of ticking hours to its credit. It had a long pendulum and two weights. Every thirty minutes its deep, beautiful chiming reverberated through the house. It belonged to that family of clocks that insisted time was deliberate in its passing.

July 30th — The day before yesterday we moved into our new hideout in the stable. In its cellar the door separating the two "rooms" was taken off its hinges and moved away and they built a wall in its place. That's it, we have a hideout. The entrance is under the late lamented door and it's shaped like the letter L. The girls and I don't have any problem with it but the adults have difficulty passing through. They built benches covered with fodder and straw and we sleep on them and also spend our time there when the hideout is closed. When it's open we can climb up to the stable. We can also sleep in the attic on the straw. Parille is there, the forester who also has found asylum with us. In the morning they bring us water, later on coffee and then they lock us in or we sit above. At noon a meal, in the evening again coffee. . . . Now the landlords run back and forth more than usual. That will break them.

■ This writing develops redundant sensibilities in me: all the time I wait for the blow. It will come. Will I know when and where? I also find it hard to concentrate, because while translating my mind experiences a rush of various pictures intermingles with strange associations.

I once told my wife how, sometime at the end of the Forties, my then girlfriend and I returned from a new year's celebration. It was cold and damp, a few streetlights stained the darkness with yellow. I clung to her, probably in an odd way, because she asked, "why like that?" and I answered that since the war I suffer from a strange symptom: I don't see in the dark. "It's called 'chicken blindness' and I don't know whether it's a physical malady or a psychological inhibition. Maybe it has to do with the lack of vitamins, especially during the period of growing up, or possibly another aspect of anxiety."

"All of you from there," said my wife, "suffer from constant anxiety."

August 8th — *It's a nice day, washed with sunshine, but not for us. Maybe some time in the future we'll have such a day for ourselves. Who knows. Yesterday in the morning Hryc came with news "from the radio" that Hitler resigned and appointed a "council of three" to succeed him. He didn't know the composition of the council. And of course it turned out to be a lie as I thought it would, just a total bluff. Like the news last year that the Wehrmacht took over the government. The women in the hideout — Mother, Linka and Edzia — almost blew up the roof, they were so glad. Uncle and I didn't believe the story even for one moment.*

■ Today it sounds funny and also impossible. Today we drown in a flood of information that pours over us. Even if now, too, it's hard at times to know the truth. Then, in those times, the whole volume of information was based on gossip. True, the speed at which the gossip spread was enormous. It could compete only with the radio, and owning a radio was illegal, the press was censored and watery. TV— who even dreamed of it?

The lack of trust ingrained in me at that time makes it difficult to read a newspaper. I always experience a depressing feeling I had already had, that that garbage is familiar. Nothing has changed up to this very day and will never change.

In the evening Parille told us that at noon a great quarrel broke out between Helena and Misia. Today isn't only Sunday but St. Mary's Day as well, and when they came back from church Helena said to Misia in her arrogant voice: "What does it mean? The potatoes haven't been peeled and there's no fire in the stove." Misia retorted that she wasn't her house maid and that she wasn't obliged to carry out her orders. All the quarrel needed was that to ignite. Karol, who hates his wife, supported Misia and claimed she was right. Helena responded in a very sharp way, mentioning to him that he used to screw Misia and that was the reason they were going to divorce each other before the war.

■ This time it was a different dream, a dream that somehow has been etched in my memory: when my wife was trying on me a part of the sweater that she had knitted for me, a big polar bear burst into the room, looked around, growled, caught my wife in its hands (or paws?) and devoured her. I didn't lose my head, pulled a shotgun from the desk, aimed carefully and killed the bear. Later I sold the meat (naturally my wife was Jewish and so the meat was kosher) and spread its fur at the foot of my bed.

Thus I derived another benefit from my wife.

Usually people believe that leftovers of reality steal into a dream. Probably not always. There are no polar bears in Tel Aviv, I don't have a shotgun and my wife doesn't knit.

So what's hiding behind the dream? Has it anything to do with the diary?

Monday, August 16th *— Today the quarrel subsided. Misia is cooking a lunch of meat that allegedly (so said Helena) she received for our belongings. Hryc picked up the leather boots at the cobbler's, those boots he received from Linka, and bought him-*

*self a new hat. He struts about proud and pompous as if he was,
at least, the village Head. In the afternoon Mother asked Misia to
allow her to go to the apartment and take a few things, but Misia
answered rudely, "Please apply to Mr. Karol." As Hryc went to
Gologory, the village of his birth, Misia probably gave him some
items of ours for exchange (without our knowledge). This is probably the reason for her refusal to let Mother go to the apartment.
She didn't want her to discover what was missing. I don't understand why she needed to do all that: she could have told Mother to
give her a few things to barter and Mother would have agreed. I
don't understand.*

■ Maybe I was cut off from reality and drifted into an unreal world.
I grasped that when I recently stood in the museum and looked at
Chagall's "The Floating Jew." He reveals himself to me time and
again as if I, too, was floating — like the Jew from the painting —
over the eradicated past.

The small boy — is it me? Running in the avenue and pushing
a colored wooden wheel with his stick. And in another scene, the
same boy, slightly older, running along the same avenue, escaping
from a German officer who wants to shoot him.

I float over decades that were shaped in those 1111 days.
I float over the dim memories.
I float over the desert of my life.
I float . . . .

*August 17th — Nothing special happened today with the excep-
tion of the fact that I managed to wash myself from head to toe,
and for lunch we had corn and baked pears. Considering we're
staying at a hideout, this is a special event.*

■ "Our hope is not lost yet," wrote Naftali Imber.[32] As a native of
Zloczow he knew what he was talking about. Without hope one
cannot live there. But how many hopes were shattered here as well
as there? I don't even remember what I was hoping for. My father
was a Zionist but of the kind that doesn't even dream of making

aliyah. When one of his friends went to the Land of Israel it was quite clear that he did it because he wanted to free his wife from the clutches of her Ukrainian lover. Still, already at the beginning of the war he argued that the Jews would cause Hitler's defeat because "if they made aliyah to the Land of Israel and didn't stay in Poland, the Germans wouldn't know what to begin with. And now the Jews are disappearing, which would make it difficult for him and thus. . . ."

Those who weren't liquidated and yet went to Israel are ghosts trying to keep a state, which floats over deserts, over sandstorms and is unable to land and strike roots. The severed roots remained there.

August 20th — For two days I couldn't write because my eyes were burning and it seems to me that I've got an inflammation. The worst thing is that we have no eye drops here. They remained in Zloczow and when Mother was in town she didn't bring them. As a matter of fact, she didn't take a lot of things because Hryc refused to carry them. Probably, if she would have taken me with her, I would have remembered or compelled her to take them. Now the eye drops will at best be lost. It's not important — what matters is to manage to come out of the war alive. I don't have much hope. Everybody is full of joy because the Soviets are "galloping," but we don't see them. The day before yesterday Sicily surrendered, the Allies bombed Italy and Germany — and I don't care. The Germans have killed so many of us that it's permissible to liquidate them.

■ While standing in the center of the Zloczow market, I remembered how as liberation seemed to be approaching I craved going with the Russians westward so that I could help rule the Germans. I learned something: immediately after we'd occupy a town, I'd post notices everywhere ordering all men to show up the next day in the central square. I had no doubt that such disciplined people would all arrive, ready for action.

In the burning sun, while their wives peeped from behind pots of geraniums and followed, all agog, the happenings, the Germans would dig pits for themselves and shoot each other.

An order is an order, but a dream is also only a dream.

Today was some panic because last night Hryc informed us about the police arriving at Kolczakowska's house — a friend of Helena's who has a house not far from us (Helena keeps the keys) — looking for Jews. Because of that the hideout was closed from morning until 4 p.m. and we received our lunch late. Helena said there were area combings, the Wehrmacht arrived, as well as the foresters and the police, and they went from house to house, from forest to forest, because Jews were hiding in the environs.

■ Here in the center of the market — under the statue of Lenin in Soviet times — was a bunker where my friend Rysiek was hiding (along with twenty other Jews). The Germans tried to reach the bunker but in vain, because the entrance was through the sewers. Even gas bombs didn't work because the draft blew the gas away. I wonder if that bunker still exists. Will its ceiling collapse one day and the market sink in the deep?

August 21st — Uncle Henryk used to have a beautiful encyclopedia of trains. Originally it belonged to our grandfather who worked for the railway. I don't understand why nobody has ever thought that it was very uncomfortable for the engine driver to be somewhere in the rear end . . . therefore I invented another, modern locomotive.

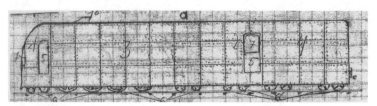

Plans for a new locomotive

■ A demagogue once said: "Can we imagine how many Einsteins were liquidated?"

Sorry, but perhaps it's not demagogy? Maybe it's the truth? Isn't it a fact that some of my ideas have been used — not by me — after the war? Would I have become an inventor if there were no war? Who knows?

At my age — it's not important . . . Stupid questions, questions without answers.

August 23rd — I don't write every day because there's no news. Yesterday we had a visit by Oleg, Misia's nephew. He said that the Allies landed in Calabria and that the German commander of Oriol came to Hitler and after the Führer reproached him for surrendering to the Soviets the general shot Hitler and then committed suicide. Hitler was seriously wounded. Experience teaches us that such stories are pipe dreams. Like all fables.

■ During this war, gossip played an important role: a morale booster. Its rapid spread served as an elixir of life, the most important component of it.

Even in "normal" times all begins with gossip. Particularly literature. What's literature? A gossip of unfamiliar people, not even seen on the TV screen. What has come out of the juicy story of Helen and Paris ? The War of Troy? Never! Who would have known of that war, or even more important, of the Helen story if Homer didn't write *The Iliad*.

Years ago Heinrich Mann wrote to his brother Thomas that he didn't know whether literature could help Man to live, but he hoped it wouldn't help him to die. Like gossip?

August 30th — I haven't written for several days because I have neither patience nor will. Yesterday I was sick. I don't know the reason for my fever both yesterday and the day before. Mother was very worried but today I'm as healthy as an ox. Last night Mother went up to the apartment to pick up a few things and coming back said that Misia had perpetrated a Witches' Sabbath [in Yiddish, "a

*schwartze Shabbes"] over there. When we moved over to the stable
the drawers were full. Now they're empty. Well, nothing can be
done about that. If we manage to go through these shitty times —
we'll have other things or just live without them. And if it's
ordained that we won't survive, then to hell with it all.*

■ To hell. So what?

Yes, that's the expression that best summarizes the complex or
life philosophy. What value does property have if it's certain that
sooner or later another Genghis Khan pops up, a new comet in the
skies waving its shining tail, erase it all.

And as my experience teaches me, we'll have to start it all again
from scratch.

Will that excite me? I doubt that I can be excited by anything.

*On the surface the political situation seems to be excellent.
Roosevelt and Churchill met in Quebec and decided to meet again
in three months (maybe the signing of a peace treaty!). And
conduct a "swift war." May God grant us getting out into fresh air,
freedom. I wouldn't have to look out the crack and envy the geese,
the chickens and Rex which are allowed to stroll in the yard, not
like me, a "dirty Jew," who must stay in the cellar, in the hideout,
depending on Misia and Helena's moods. A communiqué from the
German Supreme Command published in the newspaper reports
that "the local breaches attained by the Soviets have been closed
again by an elastic German defense." Yesterday the Soviets
liberated Kharkov and it's said they arrived at the distance of
350 kilometers from the border. Kiev is burning and Lvov is
overflowing with wounded. Perhaps the end is at hand . . . .*

■ When I was a child I liked going to the Fotoplastikon, a pre-tele-
vision invention. There they screened pictures of exotic landscapes,
strange animals and weird people. In the darkness of the small
auditorium stood a wooden shack surrounded by seats joined to it.
With your face touching the shack's wall you looked through
binoculars in which the slides kept changing every few minutes.

Everything in the binoculars was three-dimensional, even the tits of the African women or the mountains. If the ticket-seller didn't notice one could keep one's seat and watch the same things over and over again.

I can't say the same thing about the diary. It's impossible, also undesirable, to begin watching it all from scratch. It's depressing and therefore must end. Enough is enough.

September 7th — *I drew the golden Polish autumn beyond the crack — my window to landscapes far away.*

Landscape in autumn

■ This colored drawing included in the diary: sunlight, courtyard, and chickens.

The painting is very "readable," despite my lack of painting skills. Maybe the impulse for freedom, maybe the need to express myself?

For years now, when I go to bed and before falling asleep, weird faces appear under my eyelids. Unfamiliar portraits emerging from the subconscious. In the morning I cannot recall whether they were men or women. I only dimly remember that they were ugly and I find it irritating, having no painting gift, to be unable to put those faces on paper.

September 8th — *I don't write regularly because I have neither patience nor "time." I'm now sitting in the hideout in the wake of an alert both yesterday and today. Partisans are fighting the Germans at Ruda-Koltowska. The wounded are driven along with artillery, an army mobilized on motorbikes with machine guns, even tanks — a real battle is being waged. Even if it's conducted 9 kms from here — we are locked in the cellar. Why? Misia had*

pains and entered her bed but once Hryc arrived with that piece of
news she was immediately cured and ran down to lock us up.
Mother was lying upstairs fast asleep (she didn't feel well, had a
cold) when Hryc burst in, "Partisans, shooting, bringing in
wounded Germans!" I thought he meant our forest, right here, and
then luckily Stanislawska arrived and soothed him. She said he just
talked with a peasant from Ruda and everything was quiet there,
nothing happening. It helped us a bit because otherwise we would
be sitting in the hideout without a break.

■ How stupid I was! How I surrendered to the popular "roots"
fashion and went back to Zloczow! But that chapter in my life was
finished. That's what I thought.

My street is quiet and washed by sunlight, and there everything
looks different from here, from my memories. There the street is
gray, the people there are gray, the ugly houses are gray — everything is sad and depressing, as in a surrealistic dream.

On the way home, in a Polish Tupolew plane, the stewardess
distributed little vodka bottles. After having my drink my eyes
closed and shreds of dreams began galloping: a street in Zloczow
where I discovered that my fingers were not straight but rather
inclined to grow round, to always be on the way to becoming a fist;
or that place where I checked with my father how was it that every
evening the sun goes to bed in Lvov and every morning wakes up
in Tarnopol. Many similar important discoveries happened here,
in the streets of Zloczow. Did I go back in order to remember?
What?

The political situation is splendid. The British have landed in Italy
and already occupy Reggio di Calabria. The Soviets "gallop." The
communiqués issued by the German HQ no longer use the formula
"west of the Mius River" but "the Don area," which indicates
they've been retreating at an impressive pace. Maybe our horrific
life will end this year. If not, the bet is 99% to 100% that we won't
survive the winter. Indeed, no hole in Heaven will follow but we,
too, won't be there. How I crave to live, to see the world, to follow

in Father's footsteps and recompense Mother for these hard times.
To enable her to live without worries, in happiness and affluence. If
I'm lucky I'll possibly live to be rich. Maybe I'll grow up into a
human being. Maybe I'll just be. Maybe.

■ There's no "maybe." One lives or one disappears. The diary
proves when the blossoms of stupidity showed up.

Same as it's clear that there are no survivors of the Holocaust.
None was saved. There are a few remnants and all, all of them,
infected. Like atomic radiation — sometimes years pass till the
symptoms appear. That's the case with Cancer of the Past.

For example: does my custom of always sitting with my back to
the wall hint in the direction of a certain kind of paranoia? Or just
lack of confidence?

September 11th — At noon we had a visit. Two Ukrainian
policemen suddenly had a craving for chicken. So, for some obscure
reason, they chose to pay a visit to our place. It seems they didn't
really understand the matter at hand. They didn't make a choice
but one of them simply drew out his gun and shot at some
chickens. It definitely was an error on his part. He didn't know that
such behavior reminds Rex of his education at the Police Academy.
Seeing a shooting gun he rushed like an arrow through the air and
sank his teeth in the Ukrainian's hand. That one screamed,
dropped the gun and like all the descendants of heroic Cossacks fled
with Rex barking after him. His comrade was wiser. He took
advantage of Rex being busy with his colleague, picked up the
bloody gun, climbed over the fence and vanished. All of us were
excited. The whole event lasted less than a minute and the chickens
completely ignored the fact that they were about to be killed. And
on the very same occasion so would have we.

■ I stopped translating, leaned back in my chair and smiled to
myself: how much chance rules everything! It seems there's no
directing hand, fate doesn't exist — everything is a combination of
random happenings. It stands to reason that if Rex weren't a

trained dog I wouldn't have written the story about him. As a matter of fact I wouldn't have written anything.

And I remembered how, when I was in second grade, a circus arrived in Zloczow. Of course I was doing my rounds there when the big tent was erected and of course I saw the premiere. A day later, when I didn't return from school, my mother panicked and began running about and searching for me among my friends. All of them told her that I attended class but were ignorant of my activities beyond that. Only my father was unrattled and went straight to the circus. When he didn't find me by the animals' cages he turned in the direction of the living quarters. He had no difficulty in finding me by the clowns' wagon.

"What are you doing here?" I asked astonished and he replied that he had some meeting close by. "And you?" he asked. I explained that I decided to quit school and join the circus. My father said that my decision was very wise and he liked it. "But," he added, "there's the problem of quitting school because even circus artists must know the multiplication table. Therefore I suggest you study four more years, graduate and then join the circus."

Heavy hearted I understood he was right and accompanied him back home in order to return four years from hence. I remember the way home, the desultory sentences and the prolonged silences.

Chance decided against my return to the circus. And against graduating from school. Three years later the world war broke out and it seems to me that only now, writing these words, I am implementing my old decision.

September 24th — *I haven't written for a long time and I don't know why. Was it impatience or lack of will . . . Generally speaking, patience has been running out. The Soviets have reached Kiev's outskirts but in the meanwhile we're cold. For a couple of days now we've had a real autumnal cold. We've been wearing whatever we could find, sweaters, warm underwear, whatever. If we were moved back to the apartment it would be much better. We'd be more uncomfortable but at least the cold wouldn't be so bitter. Tonight there were shots somewhere nearby, but here, in the stable, we just*

turned to the other side and went on sleeping. If we were in the
apartment we'd have rushed to the hideout under the cupboard.
Who knows where it's better? The best place is home. If we ever
make it.

■ Home? In how many homes did I live? I've got a friend in Paris
who has been living in the apartment he was born in, like his
mother, like his grandfather, like his great-grandfather. Generations
in one home!

In my case the memories resemble peeping out a traveling train,
shreds of life fleeting in the lighted rooms by the railway.

Something else, irritating — particularly in a time so crowded
with such events, reality has chosen to inflict strange, incomprehensible stops. I'm aggravated by the fact that I hadn't been serious
about my historical role.

The Soviets keep "galloping." The Allies are approaching Naples. By
all prospects they are preparing a landing in France, maybe in the
Balkans as well. Will the war end in this very year, and will we
read about the surrender of Germany as we did about Italy's
surrender? In any case, in Zloczow the signs of a German retreat
are already obvious. All schools have been transformed into army
barracks, day and night convoys drive from east to west: wounded,
grain, bicycles, even cabbage! Every place that Hitler is forced to
evacuate he robs clean! I hope he will find it impossible to retreat
from here because by that time everything will completely crumble.
Maybe. Yesterday Lipa read aloud a humorous piece about a
somewhat fictitious subject, what it'll be like when the Soviets
arrive. We collapsed with laughter hearing about our landlords
sitting in the hideout and we living upstairs. Only we can
understand that. All those little things, the special expressions will
be absolutely devoid of meaning to the people outside the hideout.
Doubtlessly we'll read it one day to our landlords.

■ Is it insensibility or just stupidity? Naturally it's difficult for
"outsiders" to understand our situation in those days, particularly

in temporal perspective. But wait for the moment at which one can read the "composition" to the saviors?

In my imagination I see Lipa ready to hide somebody and risk his life by doing that. And even take out, twice a day, a bucket of crap. Sure. . . .

At Helena's last visit in Gdansk, about a year before her death, she confessed that only now she began to understand her own daring. "Then I thought there was no other solution," she said, "One must save people in distress, and you were such people. It's self-explanatory. I believe I'll be recompensed for that in Heaven."

She and Misia and Hryc were not saints. Ordinary people with their good and bad sides. "Human Being — that's a definition that makes one proud," wrote Gorky. Once upon a time it might have been like that. Possibly Lipa was right: in the cynical world in which we live one can only laugh at people like them.

Why do I say "Once. . . . Maybe once"? It's certain, not "maybe!" If we don't quickly get out of here we'll all go nuts. Already now we're half disturbed, and if it goes on like that . . . God forbid!

■ I'm afraid that the paragraph I just translated underscores my mental instability. My education, which resembles Swiss cheese, makes it impossible for me to ascertain that. But when I walk in the street and meet people who look sane, I always question my own sanity. I'm haunted by fear that the past has stamped me with indelible marks.

October 10th — Several times I wanted to write but I was often a victim of my own lack of will, lack of strength, lack of motivation, laziness. And no wonder, three months of staying in the cellar, in the hideout, without any occupation — my energy has been consumed. If earlier I could wash four floors without feeling any fatigue, today I wouldn't be able to wash the floor of our room . . . It's all nonsense . . . One can yet overcome the physical problems.

■ This quarantine we had been committed to for almost two years left — if not caused — ruins in its wake. Mainly because it had sown the seeds of hopelessness. Today, now, I pretend to do something, playing a role that I really invented for doing something (true, also for leaving something behind when my time arrives).

A man is a man only when he is useful — to society, to family, or at least to himself. Society isn't interested in me, and as to myself . . . well, really!

In that time, immersed in that terrible lack of doing anything, we weren't human beings. The only benefit we contributed was our clinging to survival. Because the only thing we did besides producing garbage, besides eating — was nothing. Only eating and crapping. Producers of Shit Incorporated.

I'm afraid we might have grown so used to it that we went on doing the same. This fear slowly gnaws at any impulse until it vanishes. Maybe that was the way of our cravings. They've vanished. And a person devoid of ambitions has a more peaceful life and ipso facto devoid of disappointments. And that is what matters.

What will remain of a person without ambition, a useless person? A little mound of earth, a grave without a guard of honor, a grave of the Unknown Civilian.

Today guests came to Auntie, to Edzia. Nobody to us. Nobody knows us. We don't have anybody in the whole wide world. Nobody. Only Mother and I. Therefore there's no other option: one mustn't give in to crises. We have to stay united. Today my heart is heavy. I'm writing almost in darkness but I must write. Too much crap weighs on my heart and I must pour all of it, at least in this diary. Why is it called life? The best years of youth have gone by and will not return. Never. Even if all ends today, it won't do any good. How did an acquaintance of father's, the Soviet Jewish journalist, put it: "Parshivaya zhizn i sabachayee palazhenyeh [A life of boils-covered mongrel]." This is my life. And if I add the well known fact that everybody is born with a death verdict — what's there to live for?

■ Since I learned of my cancer, the more I doubt there's anybody interested in hearing about that period. Or wanting to read what I wrote then and today? I have my doubts. I feel I've been working in vain and that it'd be better not to tell anything. Better that our generation be content with the fact that what had happened went by and keep its experiences to itself. There's no use passing them on. No use in poisoning the pure souls of coming generations.

And Yad Vashem[33] should be upgraded to a discotheque.

October 25th — Tonight I remembered that I didn't report how life has been conducted in the hideout. Despite returning to the apartment, it's better to record it (particularly after Zagorski told us that Rome, Melitopol and Nikopol were liberated and our chances of getting out of here have improved.) Well, sleeping was possible at both hideout and stable. Of course, not all of us. Later, when the stable mice started going nuts and jumped on the heads of the sleepers, the bench there was eliminated and the uncles slept on the forage in the attic (when Parille wasn't there.) In the morning, after all of them woke up, I would enter the hideout to arrange the benches. I would go out earlier due to impartial circumstances. After doing that, Selma or Eda would always come in with somebody's request, alternately, to give her panties. I was in charge of the suitcases, i.e., underwear, underpants, shirts and so on and so forth. Whoever needed a change had to inform me. After getting out of the hideout, washing, breakfasting, taking out the bucket of crap, boredom would begin or looking through binoculars at the passing aircraft. In that way we reached lunch, which was more or less decent (usually less!) and entered the afternoon. At four p.m. arranging the benches or going to bed or if the neighborhood was quiet, whistling musical hits from better days, overflowing with false notes that would have made the composers turn in their graves. But that was our only portion of music. Later, sleep, and while asleep, hunting big game. Fleas as huge as kangaroos. And again morning, etc. A cute, interesting life.

■ In my imagination I see the dense, dark cellar with its over-powering stench and the little, wire-meshed window, in which eight people spread along the whole gamut of age, pretend they're alive.

Somewhere I read that lack of illusions prevents growing up. Perhaps. It means that I haven't grown up. Therefore I live only on the strength of habit. And gripe as well. If I'd have taken advantage of lost time, and instead of absorbing and developing complexes studied something, I'd have transformed my life.

But that also was a preparation for life. Now, too, each day resembles its predecessor and the one to replace it. No prospect, no hope for something to change. Of course it was different when I was still working. Now I get up every morning, settle down by the computer, and again the same pages, at times satisfactory, at times repulsive. The same monotonous life.

October 29th —
There's no reason (I've been thinking like that for a long time) why the car should be so long. Indeed, I'm afraid that if what I've invented here in Jelechowice was possible, it would have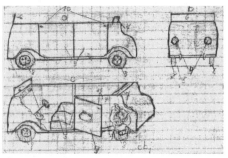

Plans for a futuristic car

been invented a long time ago . . . If the engine isn't going to be placed along the car, what's supposed to be done with the gear box? I don't know. The bumper is hidden and activated when needed. So are the lights. If it were possible to move the propulsion forward it would be possible to solve the gear problem.

■ The above paragraph is accompanied by a rather naïve and ama-teurish drawing. I don't know if my invention ran parallel to an

existing one or I was the first. If it's so can I receive the copyright
and grow rich from the royalties?

*November 6th — This morning, after Hryc emptied the bucket, he
came back, sat down on the bench under the kitchen's window and
started sobbing, "What a disaster, what a disaster." Mother asked
him what happened and he said that a baby was born at Parille's.
We didn't understand. How? A miracle? But he explained that
when he brought Parille coffee in the morning he (Parille) began to
cry and told him that a long time ago he had brought the whole
family over to the cellar in the stable (where we were staying).
They were kicked out by a farmer in Zazula where they were
staying. He carried his old mother, and his younger sister who lost
a leg in a bombing in the beginning of the war, on his back. His
second sister and her husband didn't have children for ten years.
She went through all possible treatments and nothing helped. And
here, of all places, she did give birth. So we aren't only fourteen but
fifteen with the baby! Not bad. . . . That's to say very bad. Lipa is
right saying that the baby can betray us all. We learned not to
speak but to whisper, but a baby!? What's to be done? We were
stunned and then at noon Helena came back from town and
Mother was sent to give her the tidings. She heard — and
immediately ran to the stable. We were sure that she would throw
them out and perhaps us as well. Just like that, at high noon. Why
should she be willing to risk her life further? She returned after a
few moments, sat down and began to cry, "What luck, it's a
miracle, you'll see, now everything is going to be all right, it's a sign
from God, He gave a new life." While crying she said that the
Parille family, which subsisted on the single portion that was
brought to him, had no choice but to liquidate the whole quantity
of turnip for the cow.*

■ What a wonderful taste that turnip had there in the stable. It was
white, sweet and juicy, and of course a source of vitamins. Let there
be no misunderstanding about the turnip despite my amazement

at its taste: I don't compare human beings to beasts of burden. The associations change, the words adopt different meanings, everything changes — only Man, only the human mind, is capable of creating the cathedral at Rheims or the crematorium at Auschwitz. Only the human mind can develop its first invention, the murder of Abel, into a war industry.

Helena ran out to the courtyard, grabbed hold of a chicken, slaughtered it and brought it to Mother so that she could cook a nourishing soup for the new mother. Maybe that would help her to have milk for the baby.

■ Is the title "Righteous Among the Nations" sufficient for Helena Skrzeszewska?!

November 17th — In the morning the baby girl died. Helena and Misia took a basket, put the dead baby in it, baptized her, covered her with flowers and took her to the village cemetery for burial. Another chapter is sealed in our history.

Helena said I was growing so I had to drink half a liter of milk every day. Had to and that's that. Every morning half a liter of milk from the first milking is boiled in a small red pot and I drink it with a piece of bread. Sometimes with butter that I produced — if anything remained of it — and sometimes with beet jam that tastes of plums. I rather like it. At lunch the menu changes everyday. If it was potato soup yesterday, you can bet today will be black bean soup. If today was black bean soup, tomorrow it will undoubtedly be potato soup. As a matter of fact it's impossible to say that food occupies too much of our time. Maybe it occupies our thoughts. In any case, there's not much to eat, and what we have doesn't merit attention. Yesterday Rex brought Mother a rabbit he caught in the forest. He pulled Mother by the leg toward the pot in which his meals are cooked as if asking her to cook the meat for him. Father used to say that rabbit or venison is a real treat.

■ I'm convinced that it's not a longing for any choice food but just for a plain piece of meat. The proof is that in those days I loved garlic because it reminded me of the smell of sausage. It's understandable: an adolescent who subsists on hot water with potatoes or black beans called soup, cannot grow up in the usual way. Does the fact that this very boy went on living despite all the adversities and didn't contract the whole range of world diseases mean that the right diet is not a must?

1944

January 24th — *At noon, exactly when we were eating soup, German soldiers suddenly showed up. We rushed to the hideout. A short while later we were allowed out. We found that the Germans only scribbled "5 Mann" on Helena's door — five men, and on the front door of the house 7/575. Probably some code. That way we joined other houses in the village and the neighborhood, which the Germans earmarked for lodgings for their soldiers. This visit terribly depressed us. Only that was missing. . . .*

■ On one page of the diary is a drawing of the house in Jelechowice. A small house with three rooms:

One enters the kitchen straight from the yard. On the right is a big room and across from the entrance a middle room from which a passage leads to another room. From the middle room another

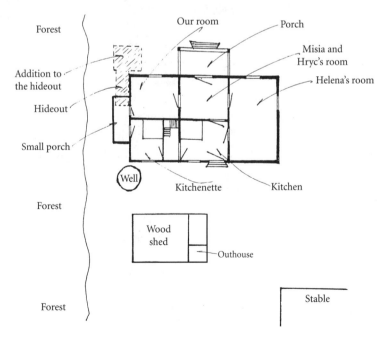

door opens onto the porch and from there one can walk out to the garden. The hallways between the three rooms are hidden by rugs hanging on the doors and covering the beds under them because there are Jews in one room, while Germans live in the big room. The landlords live in the middle room and serve as a dividing wall between eight, and then nine Jews and the changing Germans. It seems slightly extreme, crazy, and definitely incredible.

I returned to writing after a long, long interval. At first I had pus under the nail on the left hand, then it hopped over to the other hand and to another finger. The pain was atrocious and we don't have medications. That's to say, we have a little and it is exclusively for Lipa and only in dangerous cases. I haven't yet recovered from the last pus when my left arm was completely paralyzed: I was half lying, half sitting on Misia's bed talking to Hryc, when the leg of the bed folded, I slipped backwards, was terribly hit in the elbow and the arm became paralyzed for four weeks. Mother wanted to take me to a doctor in town but fear prevailed and we stayed put, which was for the better. It healed in any case.

■ I've heard lots of similar stories. In the camps, and in Siberia, a variety of maladies disappeared — possibly because the conditions didn't allow pampering. Another proof of the psychosomatic backdrop of diseases and the redundancy of medications.

To this very day I can't bear doctors and medications and seemingly it hasn't prevented me from being healthy. When my father was sick he never took pills or syrups. He explained to me that a healthy person is liable to sicken of swallowing them, and if, God forbid, that person was really sick. . . .

At that time our hideout was enlarged at the expense of Edzia. At its end they dug out 2x2 meters and surrounded the added space with logs and branches, exactly like they did with the older part of the hideout. Hryc and Bronek Stanislawski did the work. Bronek is my age, relatively educated and clever. We talked about Edzia and he said, and rightly, that she paid him for the job because my arm was paralyzed. Otherwise I would have done that instead of him and recompensed with a bit of necking. That way she'd have saved dollars. All in all she's sufficiently pretty and despite the fact that she's more than twice my age she's quite a tart — and of course all of them want it. She already had her way with Hryc, I think Lipa had his share too, now it's my turn. I'm aware of the fact that she exacts payment for . . . and there's nothing that can be done. When she washes she tells me not to look but also asks me to wash her back. She has big tits and the shirt she ties around her waist always slips down on the floor. Everybody laughs and I'd prefer that nobody sees how I wash her back.

■ Somewhere I found a saying by Rabbi Yechiel-Michal[34] from Zloczow, "Exactly as Man's evil inclination tries to seduce him to sin so it attempts to prompt him to become more righteous." Both of us hail from Zloczow, yet I'm not sure that assumption is correct.

January 30th *— Finally they arrived. We waited for them without longing. This is a unit of Organization Todt[35] — only Russians, deserters and a few Germans. Their commander lives at our place, or to be more precise, their manager. His name is Bauer. Zhenia, his lover from Kharkov, lives with him. Her doctor husband was killed in the war and her mother and son remained in Kharkov. I saw her through the window. She's not bad at all. A typical Russian. Most of the time — now, too — we stay down in the hideout. It's difficult for us to grow used to the new neighbors. And it's also difficult to live knowing that Germans live in the third room. It's hard for us and our landlords find it hard, too.*

■ There's one thing that I can't comprehend. Our hosts risked their lives keeping in their house people who were condemned to death. If we had been discovered, all of us would have been stood with our backs to the same wall. Therefore I don't understand how they dared doing what they did and how they managed to live at the same house with the Germans occupying the third room — and only one small room with two beds and rugs over the doors separating us from them.

February 5th — *We've grown used to the new life, to that incredible situation: in one room eight Jews and in the other one German. But that didn't continue for a long time. Last night when we went to bed in our room, Rex started barking at the forest. We're all afraid of Ukrainian partisans, so Bauer and his friend Gienster picked up their sub-machine guns and went out. Bauer turned to the right and Gienster to the left. When Gienster came round the corner he saw Bauer's dark shape, didn't recognize him, shouted "Halt!" and pulled the trigger. When we heard the shot we had no doubt something bad happened. We dressed up quickly, folded all up in a jiffy and went down, under the cupboard. We knew it couldn't end well for us. Indeed, a moment later Helena burst inside and as she was closing the cupboard she cried, "Hans (Bauer) was shot, Hans was shot! Straight in the heart!" We were stunned. We understood that this time it was bound to end badly. A German was killed! That means an investigation, police, and a penal unit! Sitting under the cupboard we heard Zhenia howling and the steps of several people. A car took off, they came back and I heard Helena saying, "Eto nichevo, Zhenia, nie zhurites" [it's nothing, Zhenia, don't worry]. A few moments later I crawled outside and Hryc told me that Bauer wasn't killed but only wounded. The bullet entered on the right and came out through the back. He was lucky the sub-machine gun was set on one shot and not on 75, because otherwise he would have been cut into two. I reported in full downstairs and an hour later Gienster and Zollmeister returned and said that Bauer wasn't even operated on.*

■ I've tackled all kinds of Germans, all of them in uniform — S.S., the various police, the various army units — and all of them were united by the Great Hunt; it's easy for me to testify on that because I was the former prey, at a problematic age. That hunt united them but being Germans they were unable to execute at the same time more than one action. Murdering us they could not simultaneously think. Thus we managed to escape, to hide, to survive. We were lucky because if we confronted nationalities that were less developed than the Germans, I doubt we would have made it.

February 7th — The saying "there's no bad without good" is right. Bauer is lying at the Zloczow hospital, Zhenia is spending hours at his bedside and we have some freedom. We can even cook lunches and eat. Gienster has admitted his guilt and the investigation was called off. Generally the situation isn't bad at all: because of the Germans we have nothing to fear from Ukrainian partisans and we live in a kind of citadel. The wife of the forester Antonowicz arrives every evening with her maid to sleep at our place. But last night Mother screamed while asleep and now we're obliged to sleep downstairs.

■ A few hours after my birth my grandfather traveled to Lvov. On the train he met, as was to be expected, many of his friends. He told them about the just-born baby and incidentally added: "He got hold of my finger and let me tell you, he's stronger than Samson the Hero; he will yet show the world!"

Show what?

That I cry out at night? I wake up exhausted, dimly remembering what I dreamed. A lump of lead weighs on the chest and impedes breathing. The sights from those times come back visiting with all their horror. Emerging out of the nightmare isn't pleasant either.

When I was a child I was forbidden to go to terrifying movies. My father always knew when I broke the prohibition: I cried out in the night. Maybe because sitting in a movie theater somewhat resembles a dream and in a dark auditorium I dreamed I was Tarzan? At the end of a John Wayne movie most of the men come out imitating his swaying gait.

The movie protagonists are etched in memory, at least for a while. In my case waking up destroys all protagonists of my dreams.

February 13th — *Today we really are thirteen! It has arrived in the shape of Edzia's daughter, nine years old Eva. Edzia — unwillingly — has been forced to take her in because the people at the place she was held before refused to keep her any longer. Edzia said that they were simply terrified and couldn't take the risks any more. Misia told Hryc, who of course told me, that Eva was caught a few days ago opening the landlord's fly — he was taking a nap in the afternoon — pulled his prick out and displayed interest in it. No wonder they were frightened. Edzia was right. Eva is a bad girl, acting as if she already was a hooker, not biding her time to become one. No one likes her, and that's at first sight.*

■ Of course I kept my opinion to myself. But it's amazing that a teenager reaches such a firm verdict at first sight. Years later I ran into her once or twice and certainly I cannot say anything, either good or bad, about her. I can only admit that my first opinion has undoubtedly colored our relations.

In my childhood there was a town crier in Zloczow, armed with a trumpet to the great joy of the children. He would appear at a street corner, blow his trumpet and holler his announcements. I asked why he was telling secrets to everybody. My father explained it was all right, he was telling only the mayor's secrets.

Today the Organization Todt unit took off. Our citadel is no more. Again fearful nights will begin without the landlords who'll go to the village for their sleep. We'll remain on our own against the gangs, full of fear of the Ukrainian killers, of being set on fire. . . . Again night watches every two hours, with a pistol and six bullets.

■ I have never counted courage among my prominent assets. In my youth I tried my hand at boxing. The coach said he couldn't forecast a brilliant future for me as I lacked a "fighting spirit." I do have — that's to say, I did have — a powerful punch, a high level of absorbability. But a fighting spirit? Maybe it's simply fear? During that training spell I hit the floor more than once, sometimes I helped others to arrive there, but, strange as it may seem, I remember only defeats. Why? I've not managed to carve out a career in the Israeli army either — perhaps they found out my "good" points. On the way to the rank of Chief of Staff I stopped at corporal. Not the first in History. . . .

February 29th — It's just cruelty on the part of Fate. I so much desire to cut short this terrible period, and pow! Another day in February. As if there were not enough regular days. Maybe the person in charge of arranging the calendars thinks everything is fine with us as with him — getting up in the morning, going to school, to work, and so on and so forth. Well, he's wrong. There's no reason for us to get up. We do it only in order to clean the floor from the "beds" that cover it. Thus begins every day that resembles its predecessor and the one that will arrive tomorrow, if it does. Yet Auntie dares to say, "May it never be worse."

■ The radio is playing Mahler's Ninth conducted by Bernstein. I attended that concert. The last part, the adagio, slow. True, I don't have any objective to rush to. One cannot expect a more suitable accompaniment to my thoughts. Adagio: ahead of me — nothing; and behind me? A big private cemetery shaded by the trees of forgetfulness. There, in the shade of a gray life, in the borrowed time, are buried illusions, dreams, ambitions without substance, a life that is an accumulation of bitterness, a life like Mahler's Ninth. Is it really?

I've changed. Of course I've changed. It's strange to read what I had once written. But it explains why, along with the passing years, I've lost all curiosity, the interest in the whole world. I'm afraid that loss also concerns myself.

I don't know whether this is the outcome of old age. Maybe. I've grown resigned to it although, as Shlonsky[36] said, age is not an age.

March 2nd — It's likely that finally I managed to kill a Ukrainian. But let's start at the beginning: it was during my shift at the kitchen's window. Close to midnight Rex began to behave crazily and furiously bark at the forest. The night was clear enough, and over the white snow one could see the whole yard. Only the forest looked like a dark wall. I was somewhat frightened because Rex could be trusted. Suddenly the snow became pink and then red. . . . I ran to the room and woke up everybody. A fire! The Ukrainians are sure our landlords are away and decided to set the house on fire.

■ So everything is in order: in any case we were meant to burn. So why that amazement?

I don't know if I panicked. But now, while writing that, I think I wasn't absolutely clear about what I was doing. Anyhow, after raising them all, I opened the door and like an idiot went out into the lighted yard. Two sprints brought me to the well. I crouched behind its side and emptied my pistol of all its bullets, shooting into the darkness of the forest like a movie cowboy. The first time in my life. In the meanwhile Lipa, Mother, Linka and Edzia came out with buckets. The worst was the "insulation" of needles and leaves that Hryc put around the walls for the winter. It was dry and it burned! The Ukrainians chose an easy job for themselves. Lipa pulled two poles out of the pile and all of it collapsed on the snow. We poured water on it. I don't think it took us a long time to control the situation. The fools didn't shoot at us from the forest despite the fact that we were in the light. I assume — and I'm not the only one thinking like that — that they were frightened of us being armed.

■ Always the same story, History (fortunately for us) repeating itself: our enemies always are anxious that we have more arms than we really do.

In the morning, when our landlords came back from the neighbors, they were surprised to learn that the house was still standing. Sure, they saw the flames but were afraid to return or to interfere in any way. What could they really do to help? And besides that, said Misia, you're dependable people and in any case you're here because you don't want to be burned. Hryc went to the forest and found blood stains on the snow. That's what we need, that they will return to take their revenge.

■ I hope, very much so, that the Ukrainian who was wounded then, has grown old and suffers to this very day, and his memories are the negative of the memories written here.

***March 7th** — Through the crack running between the ground and the porch's wall I see the soles of the guard walking on the pathway. In the hideout there's total silence. We don't breathe. All the time, every few minutes, we hear shots. The S.S. guards frighten the neighborhood and themselves. They even shoot at children who come to the forest to pick mushrooms. It's hard to know who is more terrified: they or we. The S.S. unit arrived in the night. Lipa who was doing his shift at the window on the forest's side, noticed the lights among the trees and naturally woke us up. At first we thought they were Bandera[37] men [Nationalist Ukrainian partisans, rabidly anti-Semitic] but "relaxed" when we heard talking and yelling in German. We thought it was a hunt for partisans, so we folded everything in the dark and entered the hideout. At the last moment Lipa said, and rightly, that it would be dangerous to leave an "empty" house. The Germans would be robbing whatever they could lay their hands on and by sheer accident could topple the cupboard and find us. It would be better if two women would stay upstairs, and so Mother and Auntie locked us in and ran to the entrance door. They hardly made it when the door was busted open in spite of the big lock hanging outside. The Germans were astonished running into them. Despite Lipa's warnings to Mother not to reveal her knowledge of German, she explained to them that they were locking themselves in the house in fear of the partisans. "The partisans are all Juden," said one of the Germans, and then asked where did Mother acquire such a German. She told him she lived in Salzburg and came here to get married. "It's all Love's fault," said the German, asked her to forgive him, went out and in a moment returned with a bonboniere.*

■ What chivalry! What a gentlemanly behavior! And always romantic. Their country was the cradle of Romanticism in art, music, and literature. They developed the tradition, they still do. Therefore they've been trying to convince the world that Nazism, a movement without a past that rose in urban sewers, based exclusively on hate, was a unique, lonely, not to return mishap of history.

And yet there are people who slander the Germans as bereft of any good qualities. . . . Let's wait for their reaction to the mounting Muslim wave in Europe.

In the meanwhile dawn was breaking and they discovered the Germans were S.S. troops. Mother says that if she wasn't hit by a heart attack she would never have one. Immediately she told them they were "evacuated" to the West. The Germans, perfect gentlemen that they were, proposed to help them, give them a truck. Auntie thanked them, said there was no need, everything was under control. Indeed. Half an hour later our landlords came back from the village. They looked really terrified when they saw Mother and Linka standing at the entrance to the house with two S.S. men. Mother introduced them, bid the Germans farewell and entered the hideout with Auntie. The hideout happens to be east of the house, not west.

■ What's that? A sense of humor? Was the meeting with an S.S. unit entertaining?

The day before yesterday I understood how smothering are the Hamsin[38] nights. I woke up tired and depressed. At the door of the bedroom stood two S.S. troopers holding Schmeisser sub-machine guns. They fired a few bursts in my direction. I was forced to stay in bed.

March 11th — *At last we're upstairs. The S.S. unit has left. At night when they came, they told Mother that they had come directly from France. I hope they returned there. It wasn't comfortable, hardly, remaining downstairs in our fixed spots day and night without even the slightest bit of movement. In the new space Edzia lies with her daughter and Selma as well. In the passage Auntie with Eda, then Mother and I, quite close. So if somebody wants to change position one has to report to his next neighbor. Our legs touch Lipa's who lies half in the beginning of the hideout and half under the cupboard. Grandma remained upstairs, and that's for the better because she's too frightened.*

■ Today, after so many years, I find it hard even to imagine that "sardine-like" situation. To lie like that for hours, for days without moving, in the dark, bereft even of the slightest possibility to talk. There was only one thing we could do and that made our life easier: the dig happened to be in sand and therefore one could piss straight into the globe and everything was absorbed. Despite that I can't understand how we managed to live in such conditions.

March 13th — In the nights, during shifts, we hear the "music" of artillery. The front keeps coming closer. Two days ago they were at Podhorce, 15 kms away! The windows were shaking to the blasts of cannon. But the Germans, damn it, pushed them back to a point 35 kms from us. There they stand and shoot. What bad fortune! Tarnopol has been liberated and we are not. Yesterday there was "an intelligence operation east of Lvov" as German Headquarters put it. What are those imbeciles waiting for?! In Italy a great offensive is being conducted against Rome. The Allies are quite close. Now, as I'm writing (sitting on the chest-of-drawers and looking outside) I can hear artillery. Maybe they'll finally move. My dream will come true and I'll become a pilot and be able to kill Germans.

■ Regrettably I wasn't able to kill any Germans. What I've been left with is a boycott of German products and a refusal to buy anything with "Made in Germany" on it. Sometimes, at stores, they wonder and don't understand me. It seems most have managed to forgive or forget. This wasn't just an Inquisition that brought about a 500 years Jewish boycott of Spain.

It's said that "every pilot loves to fuck." On the strength of that I've already made it with three. The guns have fallen silent. They fired some shots to keep the gun barrels from rusting and think they did what was required of them.

■ The impatience is understandable — and the strategic prowess as well. Every war spews forth lots of military experts of the kind that knows better than the commanders do how, when, where. Ridiculous.

It stands to reason that this is the source of seasonal lies which remain valid for some years, and then change into other, new lies. After the war I heard many stories of valor but they vanished along with the years.

Interestingly I don't remember them, but — and that's sad — I don't remember my own lies from the past either. It's inconceivable that I didn't lie. I simply don't believe.

March 20th — *The night before yesterday's the Bandera gang set forester Antonowicz's house on fire. We actually saw the flames. In the day we couldn't see the house beyond the forest but last night. . . . It's quite possible that we were next in line but yesterday protection arrived: a German military kitchen. They cook in the yard and take the food to the front. Again we have to sleep downstairs.*

■ Was sleeping in the room better? Today, reconstructing the situation over there, it seems to me it wasn't so comfortable in the room. It was 3x4 meters and had a bed that Grandma and Selma slept in. By the bed was a chest-of-drawers and at the back of the chest was a window. At night we put blankets on the floor and slept like that: horizontally, Linka, Lipa, Eda, Eva and Edzia; perpendicularly, along the wall across from the window, my mother and I. In the morning all bedding was put back in the bed and we could sit on the floor or stand up. I think there was one chair. Maybe two.

March 24th — *We live at the expense of Hitler. Every day at noon Helena brings a bucket with Eintopf gericht — a thick soup with bits of meat — that was cooked in the military kitchen and we lick our fingers. It's really good. Helena claims she told them she needed the soup for the pigs. Wait a minute, did I say anything wrong? A good question. I don't believe her. I think she screws one of them, Heinz, and I'm afraid she told him about us. Yesterday before noon he was standing by the kitchen cauldron and reading "Das Reich." On the front page was a picture of Hitler. Another cook came up to Heinz, drew a long knife that he always keeps tied to his belt, and stabbed Hitler's picture twice. A German?!*

■ It's quite clear: in the beginning they were euphoric, certain of victory, but five years later began to grow sober. It's a pity it took them such a long time to understand the madness of that man and his gang.

Last night I saw a film at a movie theater. I thought that if Hitler saw the film's titles, or the flood of American movies and programs on TV with the names of its creators, he'd have given up on the extermination of the Jews. He would have understood that he didn't stand a chance.

March 26th, 1944 / 1000 — *Last night I suddenly had an urge to calculate how many days the Germans have been running around in our space. I reached the conclusion that if Hitler had promised a 1,000 years Reich, then he was wrong. His Reich is already crumbling to pieces. But maybe he meant a Reich inhabited by people like us. The 1,000 days we've spent in the Reich are like 1,000 years. With my whole heart I wish the Führer and his admirers to have such 1,000 days. . . .*

■ It's so Jewish to wax enthusiastic over the magic of numbers! It's also a proof that the title of this diary isn't plagiarism but the result of a simple calculation.

But it's more important to emphasize that this is the proof God exists. To push me into calculating on exactly the 1000th day — only Providence can do that. The Holy Spirit hovers over the chaos of war, and finds the time to display interest in the history of one Jewboy. Chapeau!

Maybe that's the way Providence wanted to compensate me for my beginning, as the diary proves, to discover cracks and numberless errors in the Act of Creation. From there it's only a small step to criticizing the Superpower that created everything near and far. Evolution has caused such gloomy and negative results, the struggle for survival is what drives the world. All the rest is only an illustration.

Jews are addicted to numerology, the magic of digits and letters.

Mickiewicz wrote about the Messiah "that his name will be Forty Four." Why the Hebrew initials M (which is equivalent to 40) and D (equivalent to 4)? Messiah of David? Magen David[39]? Why 44 in the first place? Perhaps it's a prophecy that the diary will stop in the year '44?

April 5th / 1010 — I'll never understand the engineers who build airplanes. They don't observe birds. For example, the swallow. Its wings "lean" backward like a triangle. And I propose to install the engine behind the pilot, that way there'll be enough space for the hidden wheels in front of it. But I don't think it's possible. What a pity!

■ Years later I realized how wrong I was. Maybe, if I'd have preferred technical studies to artistic life (allegedly) I might have become an inventor. In my mind I see myself with unruly hair like Einstein's, the Nobel Prize winner.

April 6th / 1011 — I'll never put on weight. In the morning our kitchen, and Hitler's, departed. Helena's eyes are red and I understand her; I also miss the soup. She will overcome her sorrow because less than two hours later the new ones arrived: Panzergrenadieren. They installed a workshop in the yard for

*repairing tanks and armored trucks. They are better than their
predecessors in having a radio in the room. The radio was taken
out of some vehicle and that way we know all as soon as the
Wehrmacht Headquarters broadcast its news.*

■ A short time after the Soviets arrived in Zloczow the war with
Finland broke out. That was the first lesson in acquiring the necessary understanding of a totalitarian regime's communiqués.
Whenever it denied something that we were absolutely unaware of
— we knew that was the truth. So we reached the German stage
with the right training and had no difficulty in finding out what
they wanted to hide. The names of places and the torrent of words
synonymous to retreat drew a clear picture of the situation. The
underground press could only add a little.

*April 16th / 1021 — Before noon three men arrived and in the
room next to ours held a meeting of the regional command of
A.K.[40] It was funny that a secret meeting was held with nine kikes
intently listening to each and every word. They decided not to
oppose the approaching Russians and at the same time not to help
them. It was also decided to build a small arms cache under the
manger in the stable and distribute as many underground papers
as possible. Helena feels like a general. Emilia Plater.[41]*

■ She is the one from Mickiewicz's poem: she fought like a man
and when she was killed in battle, they opened her shirt and found
her breasts.

Maybe the unawareness of danger, common in children, turned
the Poles into potential heroes.

A few months before the war a group of Polish students arrived
in Zloczow for a guest performance. They were armed with canes
that had razors fixed on their ends. The goal of their visit was to
introduce some "order" to the town, namely to beat up Jews and
stand on guard in front of Jewish stores in order to prevent Polish
customers from entering. And then a group of Jewish porters, big
and muscular, emerged from an alley. The heroic Polish students

vanished as if the earth swallowed them up. No, they did not flee. They simply disappeared, and those that didn't make it in time had from that day on ample reasons to dislike Jews.

In 1940 Ionesco[42] wrote in his diary (years before his famous play *Rhinoceros*) that a new race joined humankind: the New Man. Intellectually and externally different from the ordinary human being. "I'm not a new man," Ionesco wrote, "I'm simply a man. Just imagine that on a bright day the rhinos take over. They have the morality of rhinos, the philosophy of rhinos, the whole range of values is theirs. The new mayor is a rhino who uses the same words we do but in his case those words have a different meaning."

Sorry, but I don't agree with Ionesco. My very limited knowledge of zoology allows me to assert that rhinos aren't different from other animals and don't kill without reason.

April 27th / 1032 — Once upon a time, when I get out of here, I'll make lots of money and among other items I'll order a special aircraft, serving only me. It would be able to land both on water and in a regular airport.

■ Well, so I haven't made it. I don't have a private airplane, maybe because I haven't "made" money. But today I have doubts: would I have bought an airplane if I had the money? And do I have a pre-arranged parking for my car?

June 1st / 1067 — Early in the morning lots of planes were flying westward. Helena says that they numbered several hundreds and undoubtedly were German. Maybe. But why were they circling above us as if they were looking for something and why did they fly westward? What do the Germans have to look for in the west? For sure I'm forbidden to discuss it because I didn't see them, only heard, and as a rule Helena knows everything better than me. The day before yesterday, 14 planes were flying over Zloczow, went up and down, and of course Helena claimed they were German. I don't believe that although she does have one argument in her

*favor: we happen to be in a zone of anti-aircraft guns and they
didn't shoot. If I were a pilot I wouldn't have feared them.
Regrettably I'm not.*

■ That's a dream that many teenagers are familiar with: to sit in a
plane, to intercept enemy aircraft, to receive medals, to be a hero.
And what's most important: to fly.

But is it really "only the flying"?

Or is it also to hover, to look at everything from a different angle:
from up above. It's like listening to music, reading poetry — something sublime.

Yesterday I saw in Adler *photos of American fighter planes. There
were five of them. Among them was the P-36 that the Americans
gave to the Russians. The prettiest and the newest was the Bell-Air
Cobra (P-39), all of it beautiful aluminum. It's a little slow with a
top speed of 560 kms/hour while a Mustang can do 650 kms/hour.
If I only could fly something like that! The "Messrs" and the
"Fockas" would fall down like leaves in the autumn. But regrettably I'm too young. Too old for school and here too young. Only
the Soviets might accept me as a "lotchik" [pilot in Russian] but I
wouldn't like to serve in their ranks: it's possible that a war will
break out between the Allies and Russia and I wouldn't like to fight
against England or America. I don't believe we'll manage to
emigrate anywhere without knowing languages, and without any
profession. But there's no cause for worry: we haven't yet gone
through it all and it's difficult to believe that we will and yet live.
Even if they don't discover us, what about the front, the evacuation
before battle, the heavy artillery fire? Small pleasures, particularly
the evacuation. Where should we go? We can only go, as the
Ukrainian proverb says, "Du sraki na raki [to pull crabs out of the
ass]." Better not think of that.*

■ Post factum, I'm the proof that the road to Jelechowice was the
one way kind: from there it didn't lead anywhere. From there I only
crawled on a track of constant erosion.

Helena and Misia are happy, because the soldiers would like to screw them. So little is needed for happiness! A soldier embraced Misia and already she emptied our crap bucket. If only the soldiers knew how helpful they were for us! Our ladies make fun of Misia and Helena but I suspect that somewhere in secret they envy them. It's not bad to be a soldier. War thins humanity to such an extent that the doers, the soldiers, have to fill the gaps. Fortunately for them uniforms affect women in a positive way and those schmucks need to strain less in order to win the women over, definitely less than what they have to invest in occupying the enemy positions.

■ I'm afraid that the writer was a victim to a serious bout of envy and did his best to hide his cravings by using uniforms as a pretext.

I am obliged to stop for a short while because Hryc is raising the roof over our staying upstairs and not in the hideout. I can hear him screaming in their room. An ignoramus, damn him, he just can't abide our insignificant pleasures. Maybe he gets nervous because we play "Intelligence" for days on end. By the way, we've found out that Selma is exceptionally intelligent: she writes words that nobody can think of. Besides, she's very honest, almost to a fault, without a shred of egotism. A wonderful girl! If it's written somewhere above that sometime I'll have children, I wish to have a daughter like her.

■ I found a poem by the Polish poet Tadeusz Rozewicz,[43] and even dared to translate it:

> We were very busy
> and suddenly
> discovered that our children
> are parents of their children
> they have worries of their own
> defeats and successes
> their hair is white

True, I've traversed a long road, I'm retired, my children are grown up, but it's really amazing that in spite of it all, even in those far days, I was thinking of the future. Which now I no longer do.

June 2nd / 1068 — *Recently I read Sienkiewicz's* Without Dogma.[44] *He writes, and he's correct, that Man's will and impulses are like a sea: ebb and flow. Today is a day of ebb. Maybe because Helena and Misia went to town in the morning and we were stuck in the hideout until 1 p.m. Boredom, darkness and hunger do not contribute to a good mood. Lipa found in the newspaper that Moscow has agreed to cede Vilna and Lvov to Poland. If it's true, it goes for us as well. I feel a little better. Now it is 4:30 p.m. Possibly they'll serve dinner at 6. If one goes by the English tradition it's not bad at all. Only I don't have clothes to change.*

■ Nice to have some humor left. What did happen to him? How strange is the note he scribbled years ago. I found it — funny! — in the same drawer that once contained the diary. It's written in a nervous Polish handwriting:

> *A verdict on February the 21st — Everything began on the day I was born. I don't mean that day 32 years ago. I mean yesterday. It was an ordinary day and at night I couldn't fall asleep — again. In the morning, while brushing my teeth, I choked. And spit blood. Thus began the 33rd year of my life. A verdict? I take it down in writing because I'd like to believe that in spite of that I'll read this note years later. And I have no interest in it already happening tomorrow. I don't give a shit about anything! It's a pity, the sun emerged from behind a cloud. A sudden fear took hold of me.*

The tone of the note reminds me of the diary. Strange. But one can relax: decades have elapsed since these lines were written.

June 5th / 1071 — *Mother fainted in the evening. It happened like that: upstairs, in the room Edzia with Eva and Grandma with Selma were scheduled to sleep. Linka and Eda and I went* *downstairs and Mother was supposed to immediately follow us. Suddenly I hear a noise and Selma jumps into the hideout, embraces me tightly and screams "Mummy, Mummy, something has happened to Auntie Nusia, Auntie Nusia fell down!" I rush upstairs and at the door of our room I see the following picture: Lipa is standing there, looking at the ceiling; by the couch Edzia is stretching her arms to Heaven, the girls are running about the room, Misia is rushing to and fro yelling "Is there vinegar? No vinegar!" and Mother is lying in front of the couch and grandma is rubbing her bosom with water, on the right. Seeing that, I jump into the hideout, drag out the little valise with the medications, give it to Lipa and he gives me alcohol, I put it at Mother's nostrils and a moment later she revives, sits on the couch and then moves on to the porch, near the cupboard, for air. If this doesn't end quickly we're doomed. We don't have any stamina and will power left.*

■ I've reached a state of total indifference. The quota accorded to us for life is inscribed in the divine card index; the quantity of soups or women, and possibly that of disasters, horrors. Therefore I'm not impressed by a street accident or any other tragic event. Simply, during those 1111 days of my life under a dark sky, the heart atrophied and turned into a mere weight.

My indifference hasn't grown since I was diagnosed with cancer. I definitely don't believe in the possibility of making indifference stronger. It drips into the diary and thus enables a kind of escapism from reality. But the diary draws closer to its end. Do I too?

Two things are foreign to me: being old and being sick. Now I've been learning them the hard way. . . .

June 7th / 1073 — *I don't write every day because I don't have anything to write about. It's dumb to scribble the routine of life, the daily boredom. But today the news is a piece of candy! In the night between Wednesday and Thursday Rome fell, and at midnight between Thursday and Friday the Allies landed between Cherbourg and Le Havre. At last the Second Front! Hurray! I*

*heard that yesterday with my own ears when I was covered
with bedclothes in the bed standing by the Germans' door. This
way I can listen to the radio and the communiqués of the
Oberkommando der Wehrmacht. They first announced a terrible
bombing — that's what they said! — and in the intervals
paratroops came down. Ships shelled the beach and simultaneously
troops landed from the sea. On the same evening (yesterday) they
said that the Allies succeeded in occupying a part of the port of
Caen and unloading tanks from the ships. 35 tanks were destroyed.
Not even one ship sunk! And where is the Atlantic Wall? Witlitzky
hasn't helped and neither did the bricks with the fleas of Zloczow's
Jews. Besides that the Allies occupied the island of Jersey and the
neighboring island. They also landed in the eastern part of the
Normandy peninsula. In the afternoon and before the arrival of
evening many ships appeared between Calais and Dunkirk. Maybe
they want to land there as well? They already operate from
Cherbourg to Le Havre! 200 kilometers!*

■ At a Zloczow conservatory it was called "absolute hearing." I'm
not sure I understand the term, maybe it's a good hearing and not
exclusively musical. It's possible to use it under the embroidered
coverlet of Misia's bed and turn into a listening device. The darkness, the tension, the lack of air — all help concentration. So that
following the news broadcast one can repeat every word as if it was
recorded.

June 9th / 1075 — *It's
possible and necessary
to make it easier for
people. Instead of send-
ing a telegram and then
deciphering and writing
it down, it's definitely
possible to write directly*

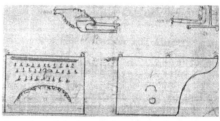

Drawing of an innovative telegraph

*and also to receive it directly printed. One has only to "translate"
the Morse code signs onto a typewriter and vice versa. The moment*

one presses the key, a precursor transmits the pressure, rises for 90 degrees, moves, "senses" a projection, falls accordingly, the balls join or separate and the wires transmit the current, the contents. The handle can be constructed at an angle of 90 degrees so that everything will be horizontal. After the construction of such a telegram machine it'll be found that the speed of stuff transmitted has grown considerably compared to the prevailing capabilities.

■ The invention of the telex, like other weird inventions of mine that pop up from time to time, caused me the same reaction in their wake. In fact, it transforms into a wild speculation: what would this State look like if all the technical minds were not burned?

If this State has arrived where it did in spite of all those politicians who think they're statesmen, but can't rid themselves of the feeling that the State is only a branch of their party. . . . Were the lost Jews different? Is it really desirable to make such speculations?

June 13th / 1079 — The offensive in the west has succeeded. Only a few days after the invasion and on the radio they already talk about the Second Front as if it is a done deal. In Italy a second offensive is on and the Germans escape like crazy and yesterday the Allies crossed Civitavecchia. 60 kilometers in one day! Here, in the east near us, nothing. The Soviets are waiting for something and I don't know what. One hears artillery but this isn't a concentrated, offensive fire. I don't have patience for writing anything. Then, chvatit, enough.

■ The handwriting is so nervous that it's hard to decipher. Only some strange abstinence compels me to continue translating. I have neither patience nor strength. True, most of the diary has been translated; still, there's much left. Maybe the heat oppresses me to such an extent? In the night I also got up and went to have a sip of water. Then I went to the window to breathe a little. It was dark, a few stars twinkled behind the roofs. I took a deep breath in spite of the air outside being as hot as the air in the room.

Standing like that I remembered many years ago when I was standing by the open window at my home in Zloczow and didn't feel cold, although it was the beginning of February. I stood at the window, the outside was all covered with snow, in opposite colors, black and white. The snow had a fresh, cool smell, the smell of my childhood. The soles of some random passerby's shoes creaked softly and pleasantly. From far way wafted the barking of a dog. The air was pure and transparent.

I find it difficult to decide whether I truly had it so well or it's memory making everything so beautiful. Perhaps it's only a waking dream and I imagine the whole entity? In any case, the memories made me feel cooler. I fell asleep.

June 15th / 1081 — What else can happen? So they'll say that another madman invented a perpetuum mobile, a perpetual movement device. Although it seems to me that it can do the trick. The pump should extricate exactly the same quantity of water as that poured by the turbine. So, does not the pump need the same amount of energy that it produces? If that's so, the whole affair isn't going to budge!

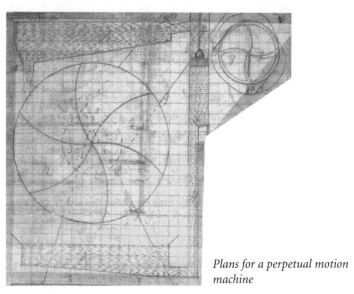

Plans for a perpetual motion machine

■ The drawing in the diary is very interesting. Such a pity that I didn't discover it earlier. I would have tried to calculate all details and build a model. Let them say I'm crazy, so what?

June 18th /1085 — In the aftermath of the altercation we had with the rest of the room's tenants, a quarrel in which Lipa said that my story about him sleeping with Edzia (it's a lie! I never said that!) was a good enough reason for smashing my teeth, and after Linka offended Mother, we decided to quit and go somewhere else. I don't know what will happen to us, for sure we'll be killed before going far enough. Does it matter? We die only once. I can't write, my hand is so shaking because of the tension. I forgive everybody, all of them. As for Edzia, God will pay her dues. Maybe that's my last wish and blessing, so I'd better take leave of my diary as well. Farewell, diary mine, I doubt I'll return to you. If not — then not. So be it.

■ I can't go on. The whole sordid scene is resurrected before my eyes. I can't take it any more. Describing hell outside plus hell inside, that's too much. . . . I don't know how I managed to go through all that without finally settling down in a loony bin.

And I hoped to carve a career for myself, perhaps even a universal one. Well, I didn't make it and was saved. Therefore my diary in the crumbling notebook has become only a private curiosity.

As long as I write, I have a goal in life. But when I finish translating the diary, what will I do? Perhaps I should use Henjo schmuck's gift and . . . ? As it seems now I won't be needing it. Cancer, as well as life on a small island in an ocean of the fighting Islam's hate, do not augur well. Clearly that's no fear (I haven't known the meaning of it for a long time now) but unbearable pressure. A pressure using a different code from the one I had been born into. And one can't ignore that threatening code while confronting the computer's screen.

Does it tie up with the contents of the diary?

June 21st / 1087 — Of course I stayed. As was to be expected. First of all, that departure was my great dream and therefore it couldn't

be implemented. Second of all, I was supposed to walk away with
Mother, so I shouldn't have fooled myself. I'd gladly go on my own,
but how can I leave Mother with them? It's extremely difficult for
me, my heart is breaking, but what can I do? I must suffer until we
get out of here. Such a pity that Mother is involved in that affair.
Well, she has herself to blame. I can't write about all that because
the blood rushes to my head. That subject — raus! out of here!
Forever or at least until we manage to leave.

■ When I was a child I saw a man drowning. He was swimming in
the river and suddenly it seemed somebody was pulling him by his
leg. He waved his arms, he might have cried out, and then disappeared in the deep.

That picture haunted me for a long time. I remembered it when
I was translating the diary excerpt about relations in the hideout.
Probably, those relations were really tense given that I had decided
to quit and go out into the unknown. Maybe I was young and naïve
and not immune, but in retrospect it seems my guess was right: if I
left I'd surely have been killed. And then, what a terrific finish to my
diary! Lots of printings in all languages, even in Chinese. A play on
Broadway with the young Woody Allen in the main role. Well, the
royalties — and they would be millions — wouldn't flow into my
pockets. Simply because there wouldn't be any pockets.

The Second Front in the west is magnificent! The Allies surrounded
the Germans in Normandy, in Italy the Germans have been fleeing
at such a speed that they keep losing their pants. The Soviets are
attacking in the north, in Finland. They seem to wish to wind it up
there. Here it's quiet. Well, in the morning the artillery was firing
so powerfully we thought it was an offensive, but regrettably . . .
Lonek had a hemorrhage. His shit is all black. He's lying in bed
without moving. I hope he makes it. I have to finish because I've
run out of patience.
    ***On the same day, at 19:20** — A terrible artillery barrage has*
opened along the front. Maybe, maybe — oh God!

Half an hour later — *The artillery keeps on. There's something in the offing. It's impossible to fire like that without a reason, isn't it?*

■ I like war movies because according to the old Hollywood recipe the good always defeat the bad — so the Germans always lose. That's the way in movies but in life only a dumb child is amazed at that. I understand the motives but despite that . . . to think a little, to express some reservation?

The process invented by Cain has been technically improved but the product is the same: murder. Probably the genes pass from generation to generation because war is still the most common and beloved of all solutions for conflicts.

When the Germans entered Lvov at the beginning of the war they found several big steel file cabinets at the Red Army headquarters. They summoned an acquaintance of mine, a locksmith, to break the locks. Fortunately for him the blow torch became plugged at the crucial moment but he could see that the "cabinets" were crammed full with dynamite. One spark would have sufficed to blow up the Germans in the neighborhood, but along with them half the town would have been blown to the heavens.

What an improvement!

June 22nd /1088 — *Today is the third anniversary of the beginning of the Blitzkrieg against Russia. The blitz was finished long ago and now they're stuck with the krieg only. I'm sitting on the porch with the forest behind me. In the east one can hear the incessant booms of artillery. Last evening a hellish barrage lasted for an hour but then became weaker. From the German communiqués one can gather that a big Soviet offensive has started from Vitebsk to Prypec and the Russians are advancing. Fierce battles are being waged at Orsha, Mogilev, and Lepel. It seems that Vitebsk is surrounded. The 10 o'clock news imparted that Ribbentrop arrived in Finland and talked with the Prime Minister and the President about a cease-fire. Helena, who heard the news in Polish, says that Ribbentrop promised German aid to*

*Finland and Finland announced it would always support Hitler.
Lipa says that he heard nothing like that on the news. But does
that really matter?!*

■ I feel I've been sinking deeper and deeper along with the diary,
burying myself in the past. Why did I need that? Nobody will read
the diary and only the manuscript will remain as a mute witness to
my successors, testifying that once there were people like that, like
me.

When traveling in Europe, observing the tranquil life of its
inhabitants, I've found what's the true distance between us. Tel Aviv
is Europe's Afula. They don't take to heart what we live through.
Possibly this diary, and others like it, doesn't interest them. And we,
bloated with illusions, think that we are the center of the world. . . .

*June 24th / 1090 — Finally Mother has talked a bit with me.
Maybe she, too, understands that the two of us can only depend on
each other. All the rest — are different. We talked about my old
love, Ruta. I decided to write about that and about other things
that happened in the past, but didn't feel like doing it. . . . What
can I do? If we get out of here I'll have, in any case, to rewrite and
readapt the whole diary. Then I'll write it all as it should be
written, in the right place and in the right order. Even today, if I
only had a copybook, I'd have started copying.*

■ This was written about fifty years ago. All those years the diary
was biding its time for emancipation. Did I mean then what I'm
doing now? Is this the way for the liberation of the past?

*I have to write everything about the Soviet era: school, conserva-
tory. Also all those things that I haven't put down in writing
because of somewhat incomprehensible reasons. To register the
characteristics of all those people who've been living with us, the
relations, the shared waiting for the end of this hell. Everything,
everything must be registered. How does it say in a foreword?
"When I grow old I'll be able to recollect." Yes, but only when I'll*

no longer be dependent on anybody and my diary will not be under hidden scrutiny or secret inspection. I'll write all my problems, worries, dreams and thus draw a picture of myself. Like I do with all the others. I'll try to observe everything from the sidelines and correctly judge them. This is the only way the diary will be worth anything and interesting to read. If I ever manage to write it well. . . . To express all my feelings, thoughts, experiences — like what flickers in some of the diary pages. I'll try to forget nothing and inscribe everything. I'll write about all details of daily life that compose the hours in this room and make them either good or bad. I'll write of all different types, all characteristic curiosities (or eccentricities). The question is only if one can write that way without being a writer! My style is not good. Once I thought that anyone who really wants anything can do it. Maybe . . . but not in any sphere. I'd like to arrive at the moment when I could open the diary's copybook and find it directly written, in ink or maybe even typed on a typewriter. But does handwriting not convey at times my feelings? Nothing can be done — order precedes anything. I have to finish because they are shouting to me from upstairs (I'm sitting in the hideout) to come up for lunch. Hot soup. I'm coming!

■ Those lines remind one of *Letters to Kitty*. Without the Muse's touch, naturally. We were the same age, the writer of the letters and I; we lived in the same time, we hid in the same way, only the end was different. A mental exercise: what would have happened if both of us were alive and met each other by chance. Would we have found a common language?

When we took an excursion in Europe some years ago we also visited Amsterdam. Of course we went to see the Portuguese Synagogue and arrived at Anna Frank's House as well. I didn't go in. I found it difficult to overcome her diary when I read it (she described 800 days) because the conditions and the atmosphere were known to me. I didn't have to see that. It's all familiar to me.

I love Tel Aviv. I feel well in a big city. True, I don't spend much time on entertainment but the very sensation that whenever I want I can visit concert halls or theaters, that I can go out and tackle multitudes of people in the street, that I can enter anywhere I feel like — that's the most important asset in my eyes. So I thoroughly understand the girl imprisoned in her room, unable to move about, bereft of Man's basic right: Freedom.

June 25th / 1091 — After the war people will be bored and they'll look for some occupation. Surely they'll try to reach the moon or another star. An idea has "occurred" to me how to build that particular aircraft. It's serious, it's not Jules Verne.

■ And here we arrive, in the original, at a drawing. It's not Jules Verne.[45] It's nothing. No use copying it.

June 27th / 1093 — Rex doesn't like bombs. Being a thinking dog he doesn't react to the U-52 or the "Gigant" but only to fighter planes. The moment he hears them from far away he enters home, whines and looks for shelter. The safest spot for him is wrapping himself around me. I understand him because under bombing I also would push my head under Father's coat. That is why I embrace Rex and caress him. He smells of fields, forest, wind. It's good to be with him and I think — am certain — he knows that.

■ Many years went by until I realized that I miss Rex. A clever dog, I'm not sure he was handsome — just a German Shepherd. He was tied to me and I to him. Since then I've never met a dog that would compare to him, a dog I would feel for like I felt for Rex. May his memory be blessed.

June 29th / 1095 — After lunch. Today is Mother's birthday. The only thing I could do was to read her the last big excerpt out of the diary. She liked it. I skipped over the whole diary and saw what an enormous job it would be to edit. Maybe I'll succeed. Edzia is sitting opposite me, brushing her hair and making faces at the mirror. Yesterday Lipa opened an offensive on her. She doesn't mind. Eva doesn't feel well and Edzia has an excuse to stay upstairs for the night. Yesterday she whistled for me in the hideout. But I, like a cold blooded fish, didn't respond. I'm afraid to go too far with her. A short time ago she told me unequivocally that she would be ready to marry me. That's exactly what I need! She herself admits she's twice as old as me, but she's at least 33-34 years old. If I fall into her trap I doubt I'll be able to get out by myself. Therefore it's better to restrain certain wishes. Maybe I'll be able to hold my turf until we get out and then . . . for sure I'm not going to be a monk!

■ Once I tried to write (as a free translation of a Russian proverb) a poem on the subject: you can't sleep with all girls, but at least you can aspire for that.

In the pre-diary era, at a theater performance in the "Sokol" auditorium — where I saw the first plays in my life — I was observing a woman who was sitting ahead of me, a little to the left. She looked unreal, fake, a pretty dress, a decent profile, smooth skin — to be precise, smooth because of the lack of work, lack of worry. She didn't seem to be interested in the play, but she was there because it suited her to be watched, sitting on a cloud of lechery and attracting male gazing, like any other horny female. She wasn't familiar to me, a rare occurrence in Zloczow. My father detected the drift of my observation and whispered to me: "courtesan." I knew that term only from literature and now, confronting it in reality, I genuinely detected (to the best of my memory) something of the high-grade prostitute in that woman. Or at least the high-grade prostitute as defined in my imagination. Maybe she was the bait to draw me to the top? If only someone like her was waiting for me there. . . .

I remembered her near the ruins of the only theater auditorium in Zloczow. It was destroyed in a bombing. Decades went by and yet they didn't build it again. And what about her? Is she alive? Did she retire? When does one retire in that profession? Is it like members of parliament?

The memories help me to overcome: Ruta, Lina. What a difference! They were young, perhaps intended for me (even if they were older

*than I was by a year) and that was an old "kurwa" [prostitute in
Polish], definitely not ugly but not for me. Sometimes I feel con-
tempt for myself for giving in, but luckily for me not for a long
duration. Maybe that's the reason she doesn't oppose Lipa? If only
Auntie knew. . . .*

■ A couple of days ago I went down to the beach and saw in a café
an elderly couple. She was having a cup of tea, he was having a coffee. They were sitting in silence. What can one talk about after years
of marriage? They had no place to rush to, therefore they were sip-
ping their drinks slowly. That way they would have more time to
look around. Watching them I could clearly read their thoughts.
"What did I see in her?" he asked himself, "short, fat, with four
chins, her width easily overcoming her height. So what if she was
called 'a china doll' in her time?" She looked at him: "He seems
dried out, as thin as a stick, bald, protruding eyes behind thick
glasses like the bottom of a bottle, and still watching girls and
thinking they notice him."

In my youth I didn't know of such transformations of love.

*June 30th / 1096 — The Soviets have liberated Vitebsk and Orsha.
Mogilev and Bobrujsk are encircled, and they are rushing along
three axes toward Minsk. In the west, an offensive was launched on
Paris. In Italy, the Allies want to cut the Germans off from the
Adriatic. Every night the Soviets bomb our neighborhood. Tonight
Zloczow received an ample share. On this occasion, an incendiary
bomb fell in the garden and melted the wire on the fence. God forbid if it fell on the house — we'd have perished. But maybe not. I'd
have gone with Mother somewhere else.*

■ Memory plays tricks with us. Despite the harrowing feeling I get,
something here isn't sincere. To the best of my memory, these are
not all the happenings, not all the stresses among those in hiding.
Is it the understandable repression? Is the reason for that an exces-
sive involvement? Or the unbearable pressure cooker in which I
lived?

Today, I don't even have the slightest doubt that some stones are missing in the gray mosaic embellishing my life. But today it's impossible to fill in the gaps. As usual, memory is unreliable, and after Proust, nobody can write on lost time.

Yesterday was Mother's birthday, the saddest I remember. Now there's nothing to be done but when we get out I might be able to compensate her, at least I'll do my best. Yesterday I decided to study algebra and geometry. I have books from Misia's collection, I made a copybook on my own and despite having no persistence I hope to continue. I'd like to know a lot, it's so delightful! I'm not afraid of work — on the contrary, I like working, work is my only pleasure. It seems to me that after the war I'll have piles and piles of that delight. In the meanwhile I'm through writing, I'm going to study, maybe I'll return to the diary later.

■ How does the old joke go? Young people think money is the most important thing and when they grow up they already believe that.

I was brought up to work. I always worked and earned my livelihood in a "respectable" way. I was never rich (can one grow rich on work?) but didn't experience dearth. I simply learned to adjust. I didn't pay the dream tax and never tried my hand at the lottery. What for? In any case I don't remember the dreams.

July 1st / 1097 — I'm writing on the backdrop of artillery sounds along the front. Not too dense but still. . . . In the west there's an offensive near St. Lou. The Soviets inaugurated a Ministry of Religion. Besides that, there're battles near Sluck. The moment they manage to break the front open they rush forward. Please let them come, I don't have any patience left. Today again I feel like leaving here.

■ When I last was in Jelechowice I realized there was nothing to look for outside the house we were hiding in. On every step, sinking in mud up to the knees, one meets random passersby with — let's call it, unfriendly faces. The neighborhood is definitely hostile.

So here you have a paradox: safety was only to be had at home, inside.

Now, on the wall above the desk, a big black spider has shown up. It's strolling in front of my eyes and irritating me. Surely a spider means a warning that something bad is going to happen.

A quarrel has erupted. Lipa said it wasn't nice on my part to spread stories about him beating Eva. It is true but he claims gossiping should belong exclusively to old maids and not to boys (that's me!). To be precise, the stories were Mother's, not mine, but what's the difference? What matters is that it was one of us. We are forbidden — of course! — even to breathe when the others whisper or even talk. Never mind, we'll pull through. I behave insufferably to Mother but I can't help it, I just can't control my nerves. I can't leave on my own because how can I desert her? I can't go away with Mother because she refuses to budge. What's left is only to hang myself. It's bad on the one hand and not good on the other! How they speak ill of Mother! It's good to know even if the heart breaks. I hope God pays them back in their own coin. I would if I only could.

■ I don't know if anybody deserves to be blamed for the tense relations. Undoubtedly the conditions encouraged the evolvement of such a situation. Still, it's hard to forget, and even harder to forgive that dense, murky atmosphere. Are those things remembered anywhere besides the diary? Maybe in time the wounds have scarred over.

I stopped writing because Helena called me from the hideout. She wanted to read us some long poem about body parts. Quite funny, for a moment I forgot all, such a pity the duration was so short. If I only had the courage to commit suicide. . . . Why should I go on living with that character of mine, my temper? That way I could forget everything. But what about Mother? She's the only tie that binds me to life. I'll stop now because whenever I think too much, I blow up. Damn it!

■ What stupidity! If I cut the cord then I'd have saved myself the whole bother with the diary, the past, the redundant memories.

But honestly: what will remain after me but the pages of this diary?

July 2nd / 1098 — A moment ago Stanislawska came sobbing: they took Bronek away. Yesterday, at the Fortress, the Germans conducted a recruiting operation: they drafted all men born between 1909 and 1930 for work in Germany. Hryc was supposed to join them but Misia forged his year of birth from 1913 to 1908 and so he was saved — at least for the time being. Now we have — well, not exactly we — guests. The three sisters Tarnawski arrived: Marisia, Cesia and Zdenka who studied with me at the Gymnasium. Hryc and the two Heinzes hover around them. Klara, too, came along with them, the very Klara who used to screw Murdi, the well-known gendarme. The best of youth! But what do I care. Either they finish me off or I'll manage to quit the area and escape to Palestine as soon as the war ends. Do you think I'll stay with my current co-lodgers? The prospect isn't attractive. Take Lipa, for example: 35 years old, the son of a factory owner who was a decent, nice person. His son is different. Despite being indebted to his parents for his education, status, everything, he never stops saying "if it were not for me. . . ." On the whole, an arrogant, cowardly, presumptuous fellow but also very intelligent and erudite. Thus he's able to more or less understand the political situation and of course use a favorite saying of his, "Did I not say that? There are witnesses. . . ." It seems to me that he loves his wife or at least has grown used to her but it didn't prevent him from sniffing on the side before the war. His wife isn't better than him. Mother says that she has changed since the wedding. Maybe, I don't remember. She's smart but a hypocrite and has a terrible mouth. She doesn't care for anybody besides her husband and her daughters. If she ever did anything for anybody she wouldn't stop mentioning it. They say that her mother was very beautiful in her youth and also thoroughly a slut. Now she's only an old and noisy witch. The girls cannot stand her. And the girls? I wrote about

Selma. Eda is different. In spite of being older than Selma by a year, she's definitely more mature. Sometimes she's undisciplined and it seems that I'm the only one among the family members who has any influence on her. About Eva, Edzia's daughter, one can write a romance in installments. A disgusting girl, evil, sucking her mother's blood. She's interested only in fashion, shaving her eyebrows (she's nine and a half!) or boys. Before coming to us she was hiding at the engineer Ortynski's at Zazule. There they turned her into a zealous Catholic, one of those who are defined as "praying to the Cross with the Devil on their backs." She refuses to help, to do anything, to read or to keep her mouth shut — she's "against" in principle. And her mother, allegedly smart and energetic, cannot control her. Once upon a time she'll pay for that — through the nose. Edzia herself is a scheming, gossiping tart, really taxing my health, but finally I don't care. When we get out of here we'll bid them farewell, but what about me? I don't fit life, not having enough stamina, I day dream too much, I'm not clever, I don't know enough. I have only one asset (or handicap): exaggerated self-criticism. I might be better without it. And so . . . ?

■ That self-criticism has existed to this very day. It's that characteristic which is my source of solace, telling me those lines will never be published. That way they'll never reach the people whose names are mentioned here and are still alive, and didn't merit a better treatment by the youthful writer. What preceded what? They and their attitude toward me or the bitterness and disillusionment one can discern in the text?

Perhaps it's difficult to accept it but I'd like to believe that if there was no war I'd have evolved from a canary-raising boy into an ordinary person bereft of irritating complexes.

July 3rd / 1099 — Today is a painful anniversary for us. But then it was Thursday. Three years ago 3,000 Jews were killed at the Fortress. Three thousand! My father died there too, despite the fact that he came back and lived for half a year longer. He returned but wasn't the same being. God, writing this now everything is

resurrected before my eyes! It was a beautiful day like today, sun,
cloudless skies. At 10 o'clock they took Father. I went along with
him. The day after I went searching for him and nothing happened
to me. My friends were taken but not me. Maybe it'd be better if
they did pick me up as well? Who knows? It's so hard to live, so
hard. . . .

■ Reading *Der Spiegel* magazine I learned that the Zloczow
pogrom has the privilege of seniority. It was the first link in a chain
of pogroms far and near. I also learned that the S.S. and the soldiers
of the 17th Army Corps of the Wehrmacht, actively supported by
the Ukrainians, perpetrated the massacre.

I haven't read diaries of that period with the exception of one. I
wonder whether the motive of helplessness is to be found there as
well? Strange how it goes on and on for so many years.

And I'm afraid it never vanishes, only fades.

All night they were firing along the front and now, too, there's some
dim accompaniment. May they finally arrive. Then I might take
revenge for the Fortress, for father, for 3,000 of my brethren. I'm
convinced I'll have no pity for the Germans and the Ukrainians.
Like they didn't have any pity for the Jews. To mark that anniver-
sary we had a visit by the Germans before midday. I was pissing
when I heard a car stopping in the forest, near by on the path. I
ran to the window and saw a Mercedes by the gate, at the end of
the garden. Two Germans emerged from the car with two well
dressed men and a boy or a girl — somebody short, small. One
German pulled out a gun and shot the men and the child. They
fell down, the Germans re-entered the car and drove off.

■ In the other, democratic Germany, the renovated and united one,
they are two nice old men sitting with glasses of beer and reminisc-
ing about their heroic past. This picture isn't a figment of my imagination but a proof that if somebody has been punished it's we.
They live in affluence and happiness because they, so to speak, were
defeated in the war.

A couple of days ago I saw on TV a march of Neo Nazis in the streets of Berlin. It's understandable and not surprising at all. But why are they called Neo-Nazis. What's Neo about that?

A few moments later Misia arrived frightened and said that the victims were Jews. They were found in the village nearby and of course liquidated. The head of the village was ordered to send people to bury them but they are still lying there. I wonder how long they will be left like that and when they'll dig a pit and bury them. Something must be done. It's summer, July, and the stench will reach the house.

■ What can one add? A cynical comment?!

July 6th / 1102 — A month ago today they landed in the west. An entire month. During that month they liberated the whole Normandy peninsula and the inhabitants there have peace. Now a new offensive is being prepared. They're taking a deep breath. In Italy, too, the pace has been somewhat slowed. They are now about 50 kilometers from Perugia. Only the Soviets are galloping ahead. The front has now reached the vicinity of Vilna and west of Baranowicze. Along the Kowel-Dniestr line there is an "accelerated combat activity." We heard it yesterday night. We hear it today. Last night at 11 p.m. an alert was announced and our soldiers are "Marsch-bereit" — ready to move. An offensive near us! Maybe those schlemiels will finally arrive? Time is pressing. Our nerves are as tight as wires.

■ The nerves have stayed tight to this very day and certainly my past has influenced my behavior. I also have retained a constant panic. That's something that today, at my age, I know for sure will stay till the end.

The ship that brought me to Israel had a blue-white flag waving atop. At first I was moved but then I found out that the flag was Argentinean.

When I set my foot on the pier at Haifa I was glad to stop being Jewish and to become an ordinary citizen like anyone else in the world. But the Orthodox take care that I go on being a Jew as well as the world that has transformed personal anti-Semitism into a political one. It seems that in the secret of its heart the world is sorry about our existence and will shed crocodile tears if we vanish from the map.

And then the only blue-white flag will be the Argentinean flag.

When the Soviets arrive, what next? I would intensely dislike stay-ing on with them! I'll have to make an effort and get away to Poland with Mother (if there will be a Poland.) Besides, I'll study something, maybe I'll manage to matriculate, will study English and go wherever I feel like, to the wide world. Here in this ceme-tery, which is always a battle ground, I don't want to stay. . . . I prefer being a manual laborer there than a factory owner here. But why should I plan? Who knows if Mother and I will stay alive and if this terrible war mill won't grind us into ashes. I'm not afraid any more; what ever will be, will be.

■ Not too long ago I was sitting on the bench in Zloczow Park. On my right, the hotel I stayed in; on the left, the main avenue. There, on the Avenue, used to be Mr. Kin's ice cream parlor, the sandbox where I played in my childhood, and where the road from school passed.

And today? Confused memories, wandering thoughts. I remembered the last scene from a Soviet play: The Whites sank a Red submarine along with its staff. Sixteen sailors wait for help in vain . . . lack of air . . . six choke to death . . . nine . . . the sixteenth wants to immortalize the killing of the staff. With his last strength he rises and writes on the side of his steel grave: 200,000,000 minus 16. And that's that. That's what will be bequeathed to History. Numbers. Statistics.

Official publications in Zloczow ascertain that two thirds of the inhabitants disappeared: Jews and Poles. One gets the impres-sion that they had never lived there. So what can I carve on the bench in the park? A heart sliced by an arrow as in the days of yore? Or millions minus thousands — that's what has remained in my town of birth. Numbers. Statistics.

July 12th / 1108 — I haven't written for almost a week. Why? I don't know. Maybe because I lack will power. Every day I promised myself that I would write, and in vain. And there's lots of news. On Sunday morning the soldiers who were living with us went off. So the news from the radio was heard at 10 p.m. on Saturday. Vilna is surrounded, Lyda is liberated and a huge offensive is going on near Kowel. Finally near to us. Indeed we hear constant artillery. Sometimes the fire, like at this very moment, is sparse. Sometimes (particularly in the evenings) it's very dense.

■ I remember there was something encouraging in the thunder of cannons. And it's no paradox that it contained hope, the tidings of freedom, delivery from prison, new life.

There's nothing more beautiful than a nightly aerial attack. Particularly when one identifies with the bombers despite being on earth among the attacked. The sky is black, full of the noise airplanes make, which resembles the rattle of sewing machines. That's the nickname the Germans gave the Soviet night bombers. Blinding flares descend from the sky, spreading a bluish, cold light. It's tax-free profit when they fall nearby: one picks up the parachutes and sews shirts of the white nylon.

When the bombs fall far from us their threatening voice sounds dim and prolonged. If they're near we hear a crescendo of an approaching whistle mounting in strength, a pause and . . . a blow up. All the glasses drop and shatter and the table is our only shelter.

It's not strange at all that we don't think of the hit, the destruction; what matters is that the Germans get it.

From the day before yesterday we have new Germans: two doctors and two servants. In the forest near us they've established a field hospital. One of the servants always moves about the kitchen, cooking and creating a very dangerous situation; we can't breathe. He already asked about the closed door and Misia explained that the room was full of old junk(!) and that's why it was always locked. We're lucky there was an alert at 11 o'clock at night and the soldiers packed up everything — otherwise he would have discovered us. Fortifications have been built around Zloczow, they're full of soldiers and rumors in town say we're going to be encircled. It's possible. If they go from Kowel southward and from Stanislawow northward — then we'll be surrounded. Not bad at all! They won't be able to evacuate the civilians. The worst is that we have no news. They do have a radio in the tank in the forest and everybody runs over there to listen to the news, but even I can't hear anything. Let's hope that when the Soviets arrive we'll know about that. In the meanwhile I must stop writing and go down into the hideout in order to hide the suitcase with the clothes.

■ One can discern a new, different note. The teenager peeping out the curtain at the theater of war looks like somebody who admits he spent the period of the Holocaust in sanatorium conditions. Maybe a pressure cooker, but not a camp; no real hunger, only depression; no horror, only fear — in short, a luxury Holocaust.

So what? Pangs of conscience? So what if it was like that? Would it be better if I were imprisoned in the camps? What's wrong about that? Is it not noble enough? Why incessant complaining?

Possibly that's the reason for my bad conscience, the very fact that I'm still alive, that I was saved, and in such conditions, and I don't have heroic tales for my grandchildren.

July 14th / 1110 — It's already mid-July and no Bolsheviks to be seen or heard. It's not really true because today, particularly in the afternoon, they bombed Zloczow and us, too — a bit. I was stand-ing by the window hidden by the curtain and saw how airplanes, arranged in formations of nine each, flew over us from the north. Over the town they executed a nice turn about to the east as if in an air show. While turning black spots dropped out of them. There were eight formations of nine and on the wings they had American stars. Not even for a moment did they break the formation and the

*line. The Germans shot at them. So what? I don't know why they
didn't eradicate Zloczow. But it signifies something, does it not?
Even now, while I'm writing, I hear the howl of the attacking
"Ivans." It's hard to say that this orchestra, the melody of the bom-
bardment, isn't pleasant to the ear even if, at the very same time,
it's a little scary. Once it was said that I'm musical(?), so let me
state that I find the drums of the bursting bombs, the staccato of
the machine guns, the flutes and saxophones of the falling bombs
— and all that conducted by the baton of a Soviet pilot — just
magnificent! With Zloczow in the backdrop it's possible to paint a
new picture titled "Clouds of Smoke Drifting" but this time not by
Chelmonski[46] but by a combat painter, a fighting artist. I have to
wind up because I must go down to the hideout and make the beds
there. The "Ivan" over us is howling like a madman.*

■ Zloczow was the distant misty dream that turned into a memory
loaded reality. I don't know if it was a beautiful town. I was born
there, grew up there, lived there for years and therefore I don't have
the tourist kind of observation which is needed for such a judg-
ment. But now, following the visit, I know: it hasn't even a shred of
grace. Instead of the bombed out houses they built ugly, sad, dark
gray painted houses. The only colored spot are the red bricks
emerging from under the peeling plaster.

The four days of my visit there resembled the 1111 days of the
diary. A redundant return to the past. I can take the risk and say —
despite the English phrase "never say never" — that I'll never return
to Zloczow. What for?

*July 15th / 1111 — My writing is accompanied by the sounds of
bombing. All day the thuds never stopped. We stay all the time in
that hideout grave of ours. It also serves as an air raid shelter.
Zloczow was burning all night and now, too, one can see spirals of
smoke. Those wounded by the bombing were brought to the
hospital, our Stabs-Artzt. The stable was filled to capacity and then
the overflow were moved somewhere else. There's a dense traffic on
the road and of course the Soviets keep it company without a*

*break. All the time the rat-a-tat of machine guns firing from the
airplanes and the boom-booms of bombs. The aircraft over us howl
as if in a funeral. They play a mourning march for Hitler.
Everybody has the impression that the Bolsheviks will be coming
any moment now. Perhaps. . . ? In any case tonight the artillery
sounded very close, so close that Lipa thinks the front is only a few
kilometers away from us. Maybe they are tiptoeing without
shooting in order to present us with a nice surprise? I don't believe
it. Even if the bombing seems like a preparation for an offensive.
The worst is not having any fresh news. Why doesn't this doctor
have a radio? It's howling tra-ta-ta. I've to finish.*

July 16th 1944 — *THE BOLSHEVIKS HAVE ARRIVED!!!*

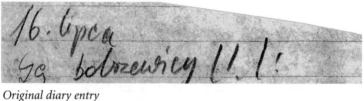

Original diary entry

Three exclamation marks, and this phrase is the only one written in
red (pencil) in the diary.

July 18th — *At 11 p.m. the doctors escaped (through the
window!) along with the hospital. At 1 a.m. we saw a pink rocket
and the first Soviet tank stopped by the gate. We didn't see
anything, only heard. I saw the first Russian only in the morning,
the day before yesterday. There was a drizzle and he, wrapped up
in a tent-coat, stood before the tree and shouted to somebody
"Davai nazad" [turn backward]! That was that! It sounded like a
choir of angels in Heaven. Finally they came. Before evening
descended, after a ten-hour battle, peace and it turned quiet. In
our garden — a tradition, isn't it? — the medical unit settled
down. We came out. WE CAME OUT. Tanks rushed by the
house, troop carriers, guns, trucks. Is the main road held by the*

Germans? God! Can anyone imagine what I'm feeling? Getting
out of this jail means the end. The final end. And now we are
free!

■ Freedom is air, it's sun and birds, it's the ability to do whatever
you feel like doing. At least it's like that on the first day. Today,
retrospectively, I know how many dreams of my youth haven't
materialized, to what extent I've failed in achieving something of all
the goals I had set myself.

The Soviet officers (with epaulettes) talked to us! But they couldn't
understand why we were white with blue spots. Lipa explained to
them that it was the result of lack of sun and an overdose of fleas.
He only forgot how to say "flea" in Russian. A miracle! I remem-
bered: blocha, blocha! I turned back, entered the house, came out
again. Only a Jewish survivor like me would understand that! And
the army, what an army! Those from the first line, all of them
armed with sub-machine guns, healthy, strong, well dressed. This
isn't the army of '41. And how many tanks! Most of them T-34s. I
also saw the new, beautiful, impressive "Joseph Stalin"! It stopped
by the gate and the staff put on an antennae. Out of the tank came
a blond woman crew member with slanting eyes. Beautiful. Hryc
stood there, swallowed his spittle and couldn't tear himself away.
The members of that tank's crew either stand in line or get into fist
fights. I understand them.

■ How the mood of the writing changed! Everything was forgotten, the bothering, unbearable people stepped aside, the world
seemed as beautiful as the blond girl on the tank.
     Only years later, now, I discovered how far that pink picture of
freedom was from reality.

July 22nd — Such a thing even we hadn't seen. After returning
home I entered the hideout to get the suitcases out, also the other
things we had hidden. Coming out I was completely black: covered

with fleas. I was lucky in carefully entering the hideout only in my briefs. I ran to the well, and Lipa poured several buckets of water over me. Everybody laughed, only the Soviet officers didn't understand the reason for the jubilation. Even among the pages of this diary thrived hundreds or thousands of fleas. From where did they come? Can it be they multiply so much in a few days? We escaped from the house only three days ago. We were liberated only a week ago! On the third day after the liberation Mother, Auntie and I went to town. Zloczow made a terrible impression on us. Only bombed, burnt houses, torn wires on the road. A mass of troops on the way to Lvov. Our house is burnt. The neighbors — who couldn't really understand how we managed to survive — said that the Germans set the house on fire because it contained the archives of the Gestapo. In the house, which was inhabited by the Gestapo unit, we found our dining room furniture in one of the rooms. It looked strange to me. That's precisely what we need: a big table, or a buffet. . . .

■ Our photographed life history was hidden under the roof beams and naturally was burnt along with the house. That didn't impede me from mentally registering all those pieces of furniture. Each and every item of the bedroom a la this Louis and that Louis; the whole weight of the dark dining room. . . . What a warehouse of junk occupies the memory! Why can't we erase redundant things, all that garbage of the mind? And like Sherlock Holmes think only of the really important subjects? For what purpose all those dead figures from the distant past crawl in the wake of the furniture: schoolmates, aunts and uncles, remote relatives, unidentified faces? Why is my head filled with redundant items? Particularly since I've been writing those ghosts have been bullying me.

We haven't met Jews. Which was to be expected. We returned home rather quickly. On the way a Russian captain, tall, with a huge fair mustache and blue eyes, stopped us. He said that he saw we were Jews and he also was Jewish (but nobody knew of that). He gave us canned food, flour, and said that near Zloczow six German divisions were encircled and they were trying to break out through the Russian lines and cross the town onto the Lvov road. It was a matter of hours!

■ I met him again in our present life. Two years later, on a street in Bytom, I was stopped by a polkovnik (colonel) who was walking with a young, thin and introspective man. "Let me introduce you to my son," he said. I was moved by the very fact that he recognized me. He asked about Mother and Auntie and added that his son was here "in a kibbutz, on the way to Palestine." We talked a bit and then took our leave. It's possible that he lives by me but regrettably I don't know his name, only that he was from Zhitomir and preferred not to acknowledge his Jewishness in the Soviet paradise.

We walked rapidly under a shower of shells and as soon as we arrived we decided to escape eastward, into the depth of the front. We picked up only carriable things and walked. Two hours later we stopped. It wasn't easy to move against the current of an army galloping westward through the forest among firing guns and Katyusha rocket launchers that kept changing their position after each salvo. We stopped at some deserted house on a hill and fell asleep. A day later, in the late morning, the Soviets broke the German counterattack and started leading German prisoners. I acquired a friend, a tankist polkovnik, who told me about his son who was living in Moscow and was my own age. In his company I would go down to the "road" and closely observe every group of prisoners. Their guards, riding horses, their arms covered with watches, would halt the Germans near our position to let them drink water from a fountain. Already in the first group I saw "acquaintances" — the two doctors who were recently living at our place. The S.S. troops were only Ukrainians.

■ Among them, too, I saw an "acquaintance." I met him two years earlier, when I came to his store, which he "inherited" from Jews. I wanted to buy a battery for a flashlight before we moved over to the village. He didn't respond to my "Good Morning" and immediately asked what I wanted. When I explained he took the proper battery out of the drawer, held it in his left hand and slapped my face with the right one.

The only slap in my life. I hope that in the Soviet captivity that slap was paid back to him with interest. As a merchant he would have understood. I have no doubt on that head.

My polkovnik friend explained to me that Stalin ordered them to hang every S.S. trooper taken prisoner by the Russians, but who had the time and patience to do that? So the guards just shoot them. And right they were, 100 percent. Many thousands that remained encircled were taken eastward. The following day, as the danger evaporated, we decided to return home. All along the road were corpses of Germans who died of their wounds or were shot by the side of the road. It's funny but the stones of that road led to the mass grave of the Zloczow Ghetto one year ago.

■ Even today I like that picture which resembles the one from *Kaputt* by Malaparte[47] — road stones made of German corpses leading to the Jewish grave.

Approaching the gate we heard Rex barking. He sensed us, jumped on me, threw me down, started biting and rolling me over. He was so glad he lost control. I embraced him, we kissed each other and only then he let me get up on my feet and come in. I hope that tomorrow or the day after tomorrow we'll return to Zloczow. Enough with Jelechowice. Enough with the peaceful life of the village. . . .

■ Nietzsche wrote in *Zarathustra* that sunset augurs tomorrow. Very optimistic. Because if tomorrow exists for me, then it's near. There's only a page and a half left of the diary. I'm about to finish.

The translation and the added writing took lots of time. I think more than an extra 1111 days. Writing became longer because, first of all, I had plenty of time and, second of all, because I had to cope with the memories and make my peace with the past. I like sitting like that in front of the computer screen; I like watching how it becomes covered with black bugs that turn into words, sentences. I enjoy that despite the difficulty in picking the right words to express misty thoughts. I enjoy despite the inhibitive self-criticism. I prefer pegging my own ideas on to great authorities and quoting Rousseau. He confessed that the thoughts found it very hard to arrange their ranks in his mind: they wandered about, became mixed, and made writing difficult. His handwriting too was chaotic, the lines scratched out, confused, hard to decipher, all of that bearing witness to the suffering entailed in the writing. He was forced to copy every page several times until it became readable. I rest my case; it's as if he was peeping from behind my back and seeing how I was working.

It makes sense that over such a long period one is able to write *War and Peace*. Maybe. But it's not enough to determine to write in order to become a writer. Especially when under my eyelids are little unimportant pictures from daily life. I neither witnessed big battles nor noticed mighty outbursts of emotion; I was just a miserable extra on the stage of contemporary theater. Probably it's too late to change professions: Grandma Moses was a one and only — also she didn't write but painted.

July 28th — I don't know why I returned to the diary. Perhaps because of feeling responsible to somehow bring it to an end or fill in gaps so that I could, in years to come, remember things that I'd certainly forget if it were not there. We live, we're free and also settled. We have a room, I even found a bed and cupboard that belonged to us. I paid a visit to my friend Captain Sandomirski from Leningrad and there, at his place and to our joint amazement, were our pieces of furniture. For sure the landlords couldn't explain how all those pieces arrived at their house. Our room is not tops but what matters is that it has a grand piano that I found in the bombed-out back part of the house. Indeed, it has no legs but I got three stools from Lipa, which we placed it on, and it doesn't feel the difference. I managed to tune it to some extent by using pliers and one can definitely play on it. The windows are

covered with boards and I'm partially to blame for that. When
after the liberation we entered the apartment of the Gestapo unit,
in the room where the furniture that used to be ours stood, I found
a big portrait of Hitler hanging on the wall. And I, an idiot, I don't
know why, threw a chair at it. The picture fell down and of course
it shattered. Throughout the town one can't find a whole window
and I could have used Hitler for better objectives. For sure it would
have been enough for a window and a half. And so the room is
always dark.

■ The idea to use Hitler cover a shuttered window seems brilliant
to me. Because what else has remained of him? The ashes of millions that scattered in the wind and are insignificant to the best of
my knowledge.

Walking in the street I met Bolek Ostrowski and Staszek Osadczuk.
They were greatly amazed when they saw me. "Are you alive?" they
asked with a kind of blaming look. I beg your pardon! Mother and
Linka started running a restaurant at the train station. So we'll
have something to eat. I'm in charge of the alcohol supply. Mr.
Imber came to Mother and told her that tomorrow is the first
holiday after liberation, the Tish'ah b'av[48] *and all the people will*
gather at Schmierer's house, not far from the Great Synagogue. The
synagogue was transformed by the Germans into a warehouse of
building materials. That had not had been the goal of its founder,
King Sobieski's[49] *father.*

■ In my visit to Zloczow I discovered that in place of the 17th
century "Great Synagogue" there is mud. The locals dismantled
the ancient synagogue into building materials. Only "Bathhouses'
Street" still exists, the only testimonial for the existence of a
"mikveh" [ritual purification bath] on that site.

I have a searing account to settle with God, an account
composed of 1111 clauses. This, despite the assumption that if He
really exists and He's the one who gave me life, He was fully entitled
to treat it as His property and throw it away as He, in fact, did. He

didn't even bother to make straight what He had done crooked, namely, erase the 1111 days from my life. It's a pity because He could have surely transformed me into an another being.

Once, in my childhood, I believed in God. I knew there was somebody or something high above that was always ready to help, having no other worries but to listen to my requests. As a child I even prayed every evening before sleep. I used to close my eyes, lay a fist on my heart — a motion that I saw at the synagogue — and mutter a prayer whose formula was "Lord, grant health and happiness to Mother, Father, me . . ." etc., all in all a few sentences.

With that backdrop I had no effort in executing a little turn and under the pressure of my saviors to become a Christian. Faith is faith and repentance is a famous and well tried asylum. Not to mention a Jew whose crucifixion many years ago had laid the foundation for a new Faith. I lived in an era in which the crucifixion of millions of Jews didn't lay anything. Definitely not a faith in other people.

What a pity that it didn't evolve in a different way and I didn't cling to my Christianity. For sure I would have attained the rank of cardinal and could have talked with the Pope without a translator. What a pity!

I even know where Schmierer's apartment is. His daughter Lina was a friend of mine and was liquidated exactly a year ago when the Witlizky Camp was erased. Today I think I was in love with her, but it made no difference because then she was in love with Uri who was, at the very beginning, slaughtered by our Ukrainian friends. Mother presses me to go with her tomorrow for the prayer. She must think that such things will prevent me from converting to Christianity. She's absolutely wrong.

■ I read somewhere that the real Aliyah [50] begins at the moment one starts writing in Hebrew. I'm not sure it's not another generalization and therefore its validity may be doubtful. This writing has taken me back to the lost paradise of my childhood, a landscape from the pre-diary era. The green relaxing landscape of chestnut trees, forest of oak and pine. Therefore there's no wonder that possibly I haven't yet adjusted, and that palm trees are something exotic, picturesque and unreal for me. The writing has also caused a suspension of time and borne witness to what extent my life had changed in the damned 1111 days of the diary. I was stunned to find out how writing becomes a total exposure. Writing those pages made it clear for me that I was more sincere with the computer than with myself.

In the epic of his wanderings, Ulysses once sat at the entrance of the Underworld and waited for the soul of his departed friend. He had a slaughtered ram at his feet because its fresh blood had the virtue of reviving consciousness. Around him swirled and pushed multitudes of the dead who also wanted to gain a moment of resurrection. But Ulysses was determined not to let them approach. He arrived from far away and was waiting for only one soul.

In this writing I was both Ulysses and the slaughtered ram. My own blood revived several ghosts and like Ulysses I kept my right to choose. The ghosts that were no part of the diary crowded round my puddle of blood, but I spurned them and didn't let them have another transformation. That was my privilege — as in Homer's metaphor — of emotional or intellectual choice. Possibly the others' turn would have arrived if I allotted myself enough time. But now I'm bidding farewell to the voices, faces and images to which I haven't brought life but my dreams were overflowing with them for a long time.

July 29th, 1944 — They all came. Maybe twenty people, perhaps thirty. All of them. The room they all stood in wasn't big, men and women together. Some used canes, sick with "the Jewish malady," a kind of atrophy of the legs. The outcome of lack of movement. All stood and cried. For sure I don't have to write that picture down in the diary. I'll remember it to the end of my life. All the Jews, the ten thousand Jews of Zloczow, were praying together in one small room. I heard the heart-rending sobbing, the wailing, the "Magnified and sanctified be His great name" prayer for the dead, and the "God, full of compassion" one, and I understood once and for all that they, we, address somebody who was absent when needed, and

perhaps now wasn't needed any longer, or maybe simply never
existed. It was noontime and

Final unfinished entry in diary

■ Thus, in the middle of the sentence, the diary ends. Today I don't know why. It's reasonable to assume that I hoped to finish a chapter of my life in such a way. I hoped that the 1111 days of loneliness had gone never to return.

I have to admit that this meeting with myself more than fifty years ago was odd and problematic. Repressed memories, resurrected sights, began to haunt me while I was translating the diary. Including those that hadn't been registered because of some reason. More than once I was sorely tempted to correct something in the diary, to add or erase, but I overcame the temptation. I also was shocked to discover that the frightened Jewboy in me has been revived. It was he choosing each and every word, particularly those written after his imagined death.

The forecast has it that finally everything will be finished. Then I'll go to the sea to bid it adieu. Over the beach a few clouds will float in the blue, I'll soon sit on one of them and look down. A shining, too tight halo will disturb me because I've always hated hats. On the beach will be lots of happy people, the waves as usual will rush toward me and I'll sit on the sand and wait for the sun to sink in the water.

Waiting for the Messiah, as in Agnon's[51] stories, I'd like to live for another day. But nobody believes and I'm content that way. What remains? My own private crab ranch [the Hebrew cancer and crab are the same word]. Therefore I'll lie on the bed — it's the elevator to the eternal hunting pastures.

In Zloczow I remembered Rip Van Winkle who woke up after many years and didn't recognize his surroundings. Imber, too, if he were alive and joined me in visiting our town of birth, would have written "Here our hope has already perished." The Ukrainian poet Taras Shevchenko[52] asked that "when I die, bury me in the far spreading steppe / in a grave there in the beloved Ukraine."

But I prefer Moshe-Leib Halpern,[53] a native of Zloczow and a great Yiddish poet who settled in America. He wrote: "My only consolation in the world / is that I'll never be buried in you / my motherland, Zloczow mine."

Notes

1. (P. 13) Janusz Korczak (1879-1942). Pen name of Henryk Goldszmidt, a prominent Polish-Jewish physician, educator, and writer. Korczak headed a large orphanage in Warsaw, which he ran with a progressive philosophy. On August 5, 1942, the Germans rounded up Korczak, his assistants, including his wife, and two hundred children. After refusing the Nazi offer to remain free while his children were taken, they were all marched three miles to the Umschlagplatz, the location where Jews were assembled for deportation by train. In the Warsaw ghetto diaries, Emanuel Ringelblum transcribed a description that had been related to him: "This was not a march to the railway cars, this was an organized, wordless protest against the murder! . . . The children marched in rows of four, with Korczak leading them, looking straight ahead, and holding a child's hand on each side." The transport took them all to Treblinka where they were exterminated.

2. (P. 16) Judenrat. Jewish councils that were appointed or elected to carry out Nazi orders in the Jewish communities of German-occupied Europe. Some have argued that these councils betrayed the Jews by obeying orders, while others argue they were trying to gain time and save as many Jews as possible. The Judenrat in Zloczow worked without success to ease the hunger and misery of the Jewish population, most of which was exterminated.

3. (P. 17) Zigmunt Meiblum, head of the Judenrat in Zloczow.

4. (P. 17) A one-time levy. This levy, or ransom, was four million rubles.

5. (P. 18) Shiv'ah. The Jewish rite of mourning over a close relative lasts for seven days.

6. (P. 18) Minyan. Ten adult male Jews, the minimum for congregational prayer.

7. (P. 20) Kaddish. The mourner's prayer that the Jewish religion requires family members to recite during the first eleven months following the death of a loved one and on each anniversary of the death (the "Yahrtzeit"). There is no reference in the prayer, no word even, about death — the theme of the Kaddish is the Greatness of God, Who conducts the entire universe.

8. (P. 22) King Popiel. A legendary cruel ruler who lived in the mid-9th century. Popiel's wife Hilderyka convinced him that his uncles were a threat to his kingdom — inviting the uncles for dinner, he then poisoned them. Mice

climbed out of their bodies and chased Popiel and Hilderyka up a tower on an island in nearby Lake Goplo where Popiel was said to have been eaten by the mice. Mysia wiea (The Mice Tower) still stands, although it is actually part of a castle built by Casimir the Great in the 14th century. Czeslaw Milosz has a short poem, "King Popiel."

9. (P. 24) Camp Lackie Wielkie. A slave-labor camp. In August 1943, Jews rose up in armed resistance.

10. (P. 27) Schupo. Short for Schutzpolizei, Germany's municipal police force charged with maintaining order in German cities and larger towns.

11. (P. 29) Stanislaw Jerzy Lec (1909-1966). Polish-Jewish writer, considered one of the masters of the art of satire. He is best known for his aphorisms, collected in English as *Unkempt Thoughts* and the posthumous *More Unkempt Thoughts*.

12. (P. 30) Ilya Ehrenburg (1891-1967). Russian journalist, novelist, historian and memoirist. Born to Jewish parents, he became the most cosmopolitan of the Soviet writers of his generation, traveling throughout Western Europe as a youth and living abroad from 1921-1940. Ehrenburg and the novelist Vassily Grossman directed preparation of *The Black Book*, which documented the horrors that Soviet Jews experienced at the hands of the Nazis. Alexandrov's *Pravda* article, which was approved by Stalin, attacked Ehrenburg for giving attention to traitors and collaborators among the Ukrainians and Lithuanians; as a result of the attack, publication of *The Black Book* became impossible.

13. (P. 30) Weegee. Famous crime photographer in New York. Born Usher Fellig (1899-1968) — his name was changed to Arthur at Ellis Island — he came with his family from Zloczow to the Lower East Side in 1910. He acquired a reputation for knowing where disaster would occur next; thus his name "Weegee," which refers to the fortune-teller's Ouija board.

14. (P. 31) Belzec. A labor camp near Rawa Ruska that the Nazis established at the beginning of 1940 and then made into an extermination camp in 1942 where nearly 600,000 Jews and several hundred gypsies, were killed. Most victims, primarily from Galicia and the Lublin and Cracow province, were gassed on arrival, while others were "selected" for work.

15. (P. 32) Yossel Bergner (b. 1920). The son of the Yiddish writer Melech Ravitch and the singer Fanya Hardstein, Bergner was born in Vienna but spent his first few years at his grandmother and grandfather's house in Galicia. In 1926 he moved to Warsaw and in 1937 emigrated to Australia where he served in the army during WWII. In 1948 he moved to Paris and a year later to Canada where he lived with his father. In 1950 he had his first exhibition

in New York and made Aliyah to Israel; he has been living in Tel Aviv since 1957.

16. (P. 32) Wladyslaw Szlengel (1914-1943). The most prolific of the ghetto poets, he wrote in Polish. Szlengel founded and was the central figure of both an underground literary journal and the cabaret *Sztuka* [Art]. Szlengel died during the Warsaw ghetto uprising of April 1943. His documentary poems on ghetto life were published in Poland after the war, *This I Read to the Dead*.

17. (P. 34) Atlantic Wall. An extensive system of coastal fortifications the Germans built along the western coast of Europe to defend against the Allies' expected invasion. Fritz Todt, who had designed the Siegfried Line along the French-German border, was the chief engineer initially employed in the design and construction. Thousands of slave laborers, primarily Jews, were forced to construct these permanent fortifications. See note 35.

18. (P. 36) Ernesto Sabato (b. 1911). Argentinean novelist, essayist, humanist — trained as a nuclear physicist, he gave up science in 1945 to dedicate himself exclusively to Literature. A major theme in novels such as *The Tunnel*, *On Heroes and Tombs* and *Angel of Darkness* is man in crisis.

19. (P. 36) William Zuckerkandel. The owner of a printing house first established in 1870; in 1875, it became a Polish language publishing house , which published thousands of works of classical and European literature, as well as books for children and youth.

20. (P. 41) "Juno sind rund." Junos are round. Famous German cigarette advertisement and on cigarette boxes. Wladyslaw Szlengel used the line in the forceful poem "Counterattack" — "On the corpses. . ./let fall in a casual way. . . /cigarette boxes that said/ 'Why Junos/ are round.'" Written during the first armed resistance in the Warsaw Ghetto in January 1943, "Counterattack" is a tribute to the Jewish fighters and to Jewish heroism. See note 16.

21. (P. 44) *With Fire and Sword*. The first volume of *The Trilogy* by Polish Nobel Laureate for Literature (1905), Henryk Sienkiewicz (1846-1916). The novel is set in the mid-17th century amidst a Cossack uprising against the Polish-Lithuanian Commonwealth. See note 44.

22. (P. 44) Bogdan Chmielnicki (1595-1675). Leader of the Ukrainians against the Poles, Chmielnicki instigated and led the most ruthless massacre of Jews in the Ukraine, 1648 and 1649 — 300,000 Jews were killed, untold numbers butchered in ways that are too obscene to describe.

23. (P. 48) Adam Mickiewicz (1798-1855). The leading poet of Polish Romanticism, he is best known for his long epic *Pan Tadeusz* about Polish gentry in Lithuania during the Napoleonic War. The poem is regarded as a monument

of Polish national literature. Mickiewicz was of Jewish heritage: his mother was the daughter of Joseph Frank.

24. (P. 50) Jewish merchant. Avraham ben Ya'akov, a tenth century traveler who wrote the first extensive account about Poland. In 965, he crossed the Adriatic Sea, journeying from either North Africa or Muslim Spain, and went through Slavonic countries and further northward.

25. (P. 50) Bruno Jasienski (1901-1938). Real name Wiktor Zysman, leader of the Polish Futurist movement, author of poems, novels, and a play, *The Mannequins' Ball*. Arrested in the Soviet Union and died soon after on his way to the Gulag.

26. (P. 52) Julian Tuwim (1894-1953). Polish poet of Jewish descent, he was a major figure in Polish literature. He was co-founder in 1919 and leader of the *Skamander* group of experimental poets, which in breaking with late 19th-century mannerism, expressed vitality, optimism and praise of urban life. During WWII, he made his way to the United States (1942), returning to Poland in1946.

27. (P. 52) Yosef Haim Brenner (1881-1921). Ukrainian born Hebrew language author, one of the pioneers of Modern Hebrew literature. Immigrated to Palestine in 1908 and killed in Arab riots in 1921.

28. (P. 52) "Kabala." Means a soothsayer's gadget but the linguistic source is Hebrew.

29. (P. 58) Kopyczynce. In the early 17th century the village became an important commercial center for surrounding agricultural enterprises; later served as a rail junction and agricultural trading center. Annexed by the Soviets in 1939 from Poland, the economy was paralyzed after German occupation in July 1941.

30. (P. 62) Kilim rugs. Cheap rugs woven locally.

31. (P. 65) Stutthof. The first Nazi concentration camp outside of Germany (21 miles from Gdansk) and the last liberated by the Allies, At least 85,000 Jews were killed between September 2, 1939 and May 10, 1945. The SS commander Max Pauli was tried in Nuremberg and sentenced to death. It was in Stutthof that an SS officer invented a process to produce soap from human fat. The product was called R.J.S., Reines Judische Fett — Pure Jewish Fat.

32. (P. 72) Naftali Hertz Imber (1856-1909). Born in Zloczow, a poet and the author of "Hatikva" (The Hope), which became the official anthem of the Zionist movement and later of the State of Israel.

33. (P. 84) Yad Vashem. Located in Jerusalem, Yad Vashem is the major documentary center on the Holocaust and the Jewish people. Established in 1953 by

Israel's Knesset (parliament), it includes museums, exhibits, archives, monuments, sculptures and memorials.

34. (P. 91) Rabbi Yechiel-Michal (1721-1786). Known as the Maggid (Preacher) of Zloczow, he was a prominent disciple of the founder of Hasidism, the Baal Shem Tov. An interpreter of Jewish mysticism (Kabbalah), he reportedly delivered superb sermons. He had many disciples and his thoughts and perspectives were compiled after his death into a work, *Mayim Rabim.*

35. (P. 91) Organization Todt (OT). Established by Dr. Fritz Todt, who headed up construction of the Atlantic Wall, the OT was responsible for other large-scale projects, including military buildings, railroad bridges, roadways, and civilian air raid shelters. Until September 1939, the OT workforce was made up of civilian contractors, among them, engineers, bricklayers, carpenters, and industrial machinists; following the invasion of Poland OT members were militarized and given special uniforms to denote their status within the Nazi system. It later made use of slave labor.

36. (P. 95) Avraham Shlonsky (1900-1973). Born in the Ukraine, Shlonksy made Aliyah to Israel in the early 1920s. As a poet, he achieved renown for using colloquial Hebrew speech in poetry. He was also a journalist, editor and translator. Shlonsky's many translations in Hebrew include works by Shakespeare, Pushkin, Gogol, and Brecht.

37. (P. 97) Stepan Bandera (1909-1959). Bandera led one of two factions that supported an independent Ukraine; while his name became synonymous with contemporary Ukrainian nationalism, he was also accused of murdering many Jews.

38. (P. 98) Hamsin. Also Khamsin. The severely hot southern winds at the beginning and end of the dry summer period in Israel and the Middle-east.

39. (P. 102) Magen David. Shield of David, in English; adapted as Star of David.

40. (P. 103) A.K. Armia Krajowa, the nationalist Polish underground that resisted the Germans during WWII while being anti-Communist. A.L.: Armia Ludowa was the Communist-dominated underground. Both were infected by anti-Semitism.

41. (P. 103) Emilia Plater (1806-1831). Fought the Russians in the Polish revolt of 1831 and inspired Adam Mickiewicz in his popular poem "The Colonel's Death," which characterizes her as an ideal commander and one idolized by her soldiers and the people.

42. (P. 104) Eugene Ionesco (1909-1994). Romanian-born French dramatist whose one-act play *The Bald Soprano* inspired the Theater of the Absurd.

43. (P. 106) Tadeusz Rozewicz (b. 1921). Polish post-war poet and playwright who, with Czeslaw Milosz, Zbigniew Herbert, and Wislawa Szymborska, is considered one of the most influential poets of his generation as well as one of Poland's most innovative playwrights.

44. (P. 107) Henryk Sienkiewicz (1846-1916). Prolific Polish novelist who has a strong patriotic element in his work. *Without Dogma* is a psychological study of a sophisticated but decadent man. His greatest success was *Quo Vadis*, a novel of Christian persecutions at the time of Nero; it was the basis of the famous Hollywood film.

45. (P. 117) Jules Verne (1828-1905). French writer and pioneer of science fiction. While his best known works today are *Twenty Thousand Leagues Under the Sea* and *Around the World in Eighty Days*, he also wrote two books on space travel, *From the Earth to the Moon* and a sequel, *Around the Moon*.

46. (P. 129) Jozef Chelmonski (1849-1905). Polish artist who represented the late nineteenth century trend called Polish Patriotic Painting.

47. (P. 134) Curzio Malaparte (1898-1957). Pseudonym of Kurt Erich Suckert, an Italian writer (his father was German) who in the 1920s converted to fascism. He gained international fame with *Kaputt* (1944), a war novel based on his own experiences as a journalist. His observations centered on the Fascist elite, Nazi collaborators and high officials in countries like Finland or Romania. His account of the massacre of the Jews in Iasi, Romania, in 1941, may be the first important literary treatment of the Holocaust.

48. (P. 136) Tish'ah B'av. Ninth of Ab, the Jewish day of mourning for the destruction of the two Temples in ancient Jerusalem.

49. (P. 136) King Sobieski's father. Beginning early in the 17th century, the Sobieskis ruled Zloczow. By decree in 1654, they permitted Jews to live anywhere in the city, to trade and to become artisans in all professions. As citizens, they were obligated to defend Zloczow and had to maintain arms and ammunition in their homes. King Jan Sobieski ratified this privilege in 1681.

50. (P. 137) Aliyah. Ascent, in Hebrew, meaning Jewish immigration to Israel. In Zionist history, there have been different waves of aliyah, beginning in 1881 with the arrival of Russian Jews, whose purpose was to establish a Jewish National Homeland.

51. (P. 139) Shmuel Yosef Agnon (1888-1970). Original last name Czackes, Agnon is a major figure in Modern Hebrew literature. Born in Galicia, he first made his way to Palestine in 1907 where he remained except for living in Germany from 1913 to 1924. While the early novels are set in Eastern Europe, those that followed are set in Palestine and Israel and deal with the replace-

ment of early Jewish settlements by the more organized Zionist movement. Awarded the Nobel Prize for Literature in 1966

52. (P. 140) Taras Shevchenko (1814-1861). Ukrainian poet, artist and humanist. His literary work is considered to be a foundation of modern Ukrainian literature.

53. (P. 141) Moshe-Leib Halpern (1886-1933). A member of Di Junge (The Young), a group of Yiddish poets, avant garde playwrights, and novelists who, after 1907, rebelled against the social protest and sentimental qualities that they believed dominated Yiddish poetry and which they set out to change.

Sources for "Zloczow and the German Occupation"

Encyclopedia of the Holocaust. Macmillan Publishing Company. New York, 1990.

Museum of Tolerance Online Multimedia Learning Center, The Simon Wiesenthal Center, 1997. *Slownik Geograficzny Krolestwa Polskiego*. Warsaw 1895, Translated by William F. Hoffmann.

"Zloczow," *Encyclopedia of Jewish Communities in Poland*, Vol. II (Ukraine). Translation from *Pinkas Hakehillot Polin*, Yad Vashem, Jerusalem. 2003.

Biographical Notes

EPHRAIM FRYDERYK STEN (NÉE STERNSCHUSS) was born in Poland in 1928, "between two world wars," he wrote. "About the first I heard from my parents," he added, "the second I managed to survive." Ephraim's father, Adolph, was a civil lawyer who earned his J.D. in Vienna and was active in Zloczow's Jewish community. His mother, Anna, was a homemaker.

At the beginning of the German Nazi occupation of Zloczow, Adolph was among those rounded up, then shot with other Jews, and left in a ditch for dead. Though he survived, he died less than six months later from a heart attack. Sten and his mother remained in Zloczow a short time before fleeing to Jelechowice, a village in the near countryside, where Catholic-Ukrainians Hyrc Tyz, Helena Skrzeszewska, and Misia Koreniuk hid them, several relatives, and others in their house. There they remained under the constant anxiety of detection by random searches and Ukrainian informers — finally on July 16, 1944 the Soviets pushed the Germans out of Jelechowice and Zloczow — "THE BOLSHEVIKS HAVE ARRIVED!!!" the 16-year old Sten penciled in the diary that forms one half of this book. Sten always maintained a profound gratitude to those who rescued him and his mother, corresponded with Hyrc Tyz through the years, secured for him the title "Righteous among Nations" in Yad Vashem, the memorial to victims of the Holocaust, and visited him in the Ukraine before Tyz passed away.

After the war, Sten attended Katowice Technion engineering school for two years but left to study theater. Writing for the stage and directing student shows in 1950, by 26 he was artistic director of the Municipal Theater in Gdansk. Despite his great love for Polish theater, he wanted to emigrate to Israel. In 1957, before departing, he wrote the head of the Cameri Theater in Tel Aviv describing his situation and offering to work as a stagehand. Joseph Milo wrote back — shortly after Sten arrived in Israel, he began his stage career in Shakespeare's *Romeo and Juliet* as Romeo's father. By 1959, he graduated an Ulpan, a school that teaches Hebrew to new immigrants, and began working for Israeli Radio.

During his career with the Israeli Broadcasting Authority, Sten became the first chief director of radio-drama and then its department head. He directed and adapted numerous radio plays, introducing the work of Polish satirist Slavomir Mrozek and other Polish artists. Three-time winner of the Israel Broadcasting Authority Award, Sten moved to Israel National Television in 1971 as head of Arts and Drama, then returning to radio as head of the Arts Department of Kol Israel. During this period, Sten taught workshops on acting and writing scripts for radio plays.

He published many short stories in the daily press and literary magazines, as well as two novels: *Blessed Memories*, which includes short stories about the lives of new immigrants to Israel in the 1950s, and *Pompeii Is Being Destroyed Again*, a thriller.

In November 2003 Zaikes, the Polish Association of Writers honored him with an award for his lifelong contribution to the advancement of Polish literature in Israel. Ephraim Sten died of cancer in 2004.

MOSHE DOR, translator of *1111 Days of My Life Plus Four*, is himself a distinguished Israeli poet. Recipient of the Bialik Prize, Israel's top literary award, Dor is the author of some 35 books of poetry, interviews, and children's verses. Dryad Press recently published *The Fullness Thereof* (2002), a collection of poems translated by Barbara Goldberg; an earlier collection is *Khamsin: Memoirs and Poetry by a Native Israeli* (Lynne Reinner Publishers, 1994). With Goldberg and Giora Leshem, he co-edited *The Stones Remember: Native Israeli Poetry* (The Word Works, 1991). More recently, he and Ms. Goldberg edited *After the First Rain: Israeli Poems on War and Peace* (Syracuse University and Dryad Press, 1997) and translated from the Hebrew *The Fire Stays in Red*, poems by Ronny Someck (University of Wisconsin Press and Dryad Press, 2002).

DATE DUE

SEP 2 2008	
MAR 19 2013	